MARCO POLO

Insider Tips

BRUSSELS

www.marco-polo.com

SYMBOLS

INSIDER TIP	Insider Tip
★	Highlight
●●●●	Best of ...
⁎⅄	Scenic view

☺ Responsible travel: for ecological or fair trade aspects

(*) Telephone numbers that are not toll-free

PRICE CATEGORIES HOTELS

Expensive	over 200 euros
Moderate	110 – 200 euros
Budget	under 110 euros

Price for two persons in a double room with breakfast

PRICE CATEGORIES RESTAURANTS

Expensive	over 45 euros
Moderate	25 – 45 euros
Budget	under 25 euros

Price for a multi-course menu no drinks

On the cover: Masterpieces in the Musée Magritte p. 38 | An apéritif on place Georges Brugmann p. 49

CONTENTS

Shopping → p. 66

Entertainment → p. 74

Where to stay → p. 82

Street atlas → p. 118

DID YOU KNOW?
The birthplace of
Art Nouveau → p. 35
Keep fit → p. 40
Books & films → p. 53
Relax & enjoy → p. 54
Gourmet restaurants → p. 60
Local specialities → p. 64
Football in Brussels – a city
divided by colour → p. 79
Luxury hotels → p. 86
Currency converter → p. 107

MAPS IN THE GUIDEBOOK
(120 A1) Page numbers and
coordinates refer to the street
atlas
(0) Site/address located off
the map
Coordinates are also given for
places not marked on the
street atlas
You will find a plan of the public transport network inside
the back cover

INSIDE BACK COVER:
PULL-OUT MAP →

PULL-OUT MAP 𝄞
(𝄞 A–B 2–3) Refers to the
removable pull-out map

Laurent Gerbaud
CHOCOLATIER - BRUXELLES

The best MARCO POLO Insider Tips

Our top 15 Insider Tips

INSIDER TIP ▶ Wickedly bitter

The young chocolatier, Laurent Gerbaud, has set a new trend – chocolate with no or very little sugar. He buys his coffee beans from selected, organic suppliers (photo above) → **p. 73**

INSIDER TIP ▶ The ultimate in interior décor

Twelve celebrated designers have created a series of luxury 'fashion' rooms in the Royal Windsor Hotel – from classical elegance to pop environment, from cool minimalism to the utterly fanciful white 'Bride of the Sea', which Kaat Tilley created for one of the corner rooms → **p. 84**

INSIDER TIP ▶ Brussels bazaar

Rue de Brabant typifies life on the streets in the immigrant quarters of Brussels. Maghreb, Lebanese, Turkish and Pakistani traders sell familiar products, from CDs to fabrics, but buyers come to their oriental souk from all over western Europe → **p. 66**

INSIDER TIP ▶ Decadence from the Belle Époque

Witches' brews in Floris Bar – among the specialities in the 2,000 different types of spirits are 150 varieties of absinthe → **p. 77**

INSIDER TIP ▶ Picturesque splendour

For some rural relief, take a trip out to the Parc Tournay-Solvay, where you can roam freely among overgrown meadows, rare trees and a vegetable garden → **p. 53**

INSIDER TIP ▶ Fiddles and feta cheese

Greek-owned Lebeau Soleil is an informal and friendly snack bar serving Mediterranean delicacies amid a collection of tools and half-finished violins → **p. 58**

INSIDER TIP ▶ Tumblers but no tigers

Brussels' École Supérieure des Arts du Cirque is world-famous. Three times a year the students from ESAC demonstrate a colourful array of performing arts in a fine Art

Nouveau building – but no clowns or performing animals → **p. 81**

→ **p. 81**

INSIDER TIP **Fancy fragrances**
Customers at L'Antichambre are guided through the various stages of personalised perfume and eaux de toilette preparation → **p. 72**

INSIDER TIP **Brussels tea**
The tiny Comptoir Florian Art Nouveau café and tea shop has more than 150 blends of tea, one of which is a mixture of speculaas biscuits and caramel → **p. 57**

INSIDER TIP **Forest fare**
The Café des Spores serves only delicacies with fresh mushrooms, depending on the season either from woodland and meadow or cultivated – for an abundance of subtle, earthy flavours → **p. 61**

INSIDER TIP **Rien ne va plus**
Le Bridgeur shop sells everything for fans of poker and roulette, but it also has a good range of board games and children's games → **p. 69**

INSIDER TIP **Happy hour**
After a tiring shopping expedition around place Sablon, pop into the Bar Pixel and quench your thirst over a beer or a wine – then sink back on to cushions embellished by a top designer. The theme of the décor is in the café title → **p. 77**

INSIDER TIP **Chameleon accessories**
Pendants and bracelets, which react to temperature change, are the trademark of the traditional Holemans jewellery → **p. 72**

INSIDER TIP **Boutique hotel**
If you like the décor in Hotel The Vintage, you can take the pieces home with you – armchairs and seats, lamps or vases in styles from the 1950s to 1970s → **p. 86**

INSIDER TIP **A world in miniature**
Automatesgalerie specialises in the world's tiniest 3D pieces – mini-mythical creatures, tiny figures from fairy tales and small-scale mechanicals → **p. 70**

BEST OF ...

GREAT PLACES FOR FREE
Discover new places and save money

FOR FREE

● *The panoramic view from the Palais de Justice*
When the sun is setting, there is a spectacular view over the Old Town from the *Palais de Justice*. The huge domed hall is open to the public with no charge on weekdays, but the view from the glass lift over the Marolles quarter is always free (photo) → p. 39

● *The history of communication*
From the first written character to the touch screen – In the *Librarium* of the Royal Library, you can find out everything you could ever want to know about the history of the written word and communications. And admission is free → p. 37

● *Grand' Place – the finest theatre in the world*
The Grand' Place is regularly turned into an open-air arena for free chanson, jazz, rock and pop concerts and also sometimes for classical music concerts. You can even save yourself the price of a ticket for a concert, as performances are occasionally broadcast simultaneously on large outdoor screens → p. 80

● *Beach life at Bruxelles les Bains*
Every year during July and August, the canal becomes a popular urban beach. When the sun is shining, you can lounge around on this artificial beach, play beach volleyball, join in pilates classes or dance to live bands playing everything from electro to soul. And the best thing about it – everything is free → p. 99

● *Music students perform for free*
Instead of paying many euros for a concert ticket, you can enjoy professional-quality classical music for nothing. Accomplished students play free concerts in the *Conservatoire Royal* → p. 80

● *Step inside the Royal Palace*
As soon as the king goes away at the end of July, you can be a fly on the wall in his palace without having to pay an admission charge. Make sure you include the Mirror Room in your tour of the *Palais du Roi* → p. 40

ONLY IN BRUSSELS
Unique experiences

● *Strip cartoons as art*
You can't get away from comics in Brussels. Many of the murals emblazoned on house facades are replicas of famous comic characters. And in the *Centre Belge de la Bande Dessinée (Belgian Comic Strip Centre)* you can read the story behind Tintin (photo) → p. 21, 28

● *A foaming head of beer*
The Bruxellois love the slightly sour *gueuze beer*. If you would like to be initiated into the secrets behind the brewing process, then visit the Brasserie *Cantillon*, run by a company that has been in the same family for more than a hundred years → p. 18

● *Futuristic spheres*
The eight gleaming spheres that make up the *Atomium* have become a symbol for the city. They may not look quite as futuristic as they did at the time of Expo '58, but they still make a lasting impression thanks mainly to the spectacular light show, changing exhibitions and not least the fantastic panoramic view from the top → p. 50

● *The finest chocolates*
Friends and family will be expecting a gift of Belgian chocolates when you return home. Aficionados often choose *Marcolini* – they roast their own organic cocoa beans → p. 73

● *Art Nouveau in its purest form*
For the finest examples of the revolutionary splendour of Brussels Art Nouveau style, visit the *Musée Horta* → p. 47

● *Cheeky cherub*
Small but smart – the *Manneken Pis* is more than just a sculpture. The little boy blithely urinating symbolises the irreverence and the contempt for authority so typical of the ordinary Bruxellois → p. 32

● *The EU at work*
The political heart of the European Union beats here in the *Quartier Européen*. Watch the MEPs, senior officials, diplomats, lobbyists and journalists hurriedly pacing the streets between the towering glass palaces → p. 42

ONLY IN

BEST OF ...

● *Brussels' cathedral – a cornucopia of medieval art treasures*
Step inside the city's largest cathedral for stained-glass windows, a Renaissance altarpiece and Baroque statues → p. 34

● *Take a stroll back in time*
The elegant *Galeries Saint-Hubert* would have been a favourite haunt of the nobility and the bourgeoisie when the rain fell. If you can afford the steep prices, then you will enjoy browsing in the luxury boutiques or relaxing in one of the smart cafés. There's also a cinema and a theatre (photo) → p. 29

● *A palace dedicated to the fine arts*
The Art Deco *Palais des Beaux-Arts* is a temple to the Muses. But there are many other attractions here, e.g. exhibitions, film classics, a fine restaurant and, of course, the oval concert hall designed by Victor Horta → p. 39

● *A man-made aquatic paradise*
The *Océade* is waterpark with outdoor and indoor attractions. When you are surrounded by palm trees and pools, slides and a waterfall with climbing wall, a sauna and spa area, you can very quickly forget about the weather → p. 97

● *Underground Museum*
If you enjoy riding the Brussels metro, then imagine the network as a sort of underground museum. Almost every station is embellished with a work by a well-known Belgian artist → p. 39

● *Masterpieces in the Royal Museum*
You could spend several rainy days in the *Musées Royaux d'Art et d'Histoire*. If you like to take a piece of Brussels Art Nouveau home with you, then you can buy copies at affordable prices in the shop → p. 44

RAIN

RELAX AND CHILL OUT
Take it easy and spoil yourself

● *The city's leisure zone*
Take long rambles on sandy footpaths or through open meadows in the *Bois de la Cambre*, Brussels' green lung. Board the ferry to Robinson island and enjoy a crêpe in the delightful café-restaurant → **p. 50**

● *From steam bath into pool*
Swim and sweat in an Art Deco building – first warm up with a Turkish steam bath, jacuzzi or solarium in the *Piscine Victor Boin*, then cool down beneath the glass roof in the Olympic swimming pool – or vice versa → **p. 54**

● *Time to dream in the perfect garden*
Part of the *Musée David et Alice Van Buuren* is an idyllic garden. After a tour of the house with its tasteful Art Deco interior, wander through the magical garden with its exquisite maze, sculptures, water features and heart-shaped hedges (photo) → **p. 51**

● *An aperitif at happy hour*
A day out shopping can sometimes be more tiring than a day at work. Your spirits will revive quickly over an aperitif in *Le Bar à Gilles* on the arty parvis de Saint-Gilles → **p. 76**

● *A spa in the forest*
The spa at the *Dolce La Hulpe hotel* is situated in the middle of woodland. After a session in the spa, take an aperitif and tapas on the terrace, while admiring the restful view of trees, trees and more trees → **p. 83**

● *Be among the bobos*
While away an hour or so observing the beau monde of Brussels 'seeing and being seen', the best place for it being *place Georges Brugmann*. The beautiful people will be either browsing the shelves of *Librairie Candide* or perusing a new book on the terrace at *Gaudron* → **p. 49**

INTRODUCTION

DISCOVER BRUSSELS!

Every day a different news story emerges from Brussels and it is almost always about the European Union or Nato. Forming the backdrop to the TV presenter's piece to camera are buildings in a universal architectural style. They blend in perfectly with the formal language loved by bureaucrats and the military. But the Brussels inhabited by diplomats, association representatives, journalists and lobbyists is just one part of the city and, in actual fact, of little importance. It's true that the *immigrés de luxe*, as the Bruxellois with their typical *zwanzé* or ready wit call these highly-paid outsiders, go to the opera, visit museums, dine out in gourmet restaurants and shop in luxury boutiques, thereby contributing to the local economy. But in fact many of them live out of town in the leafy suburbs. Their grown-up children, on the other hand, live in the heart of the city in attic flats overlooking the canal or in studios beside fashionable squares; they frequent quirky wine bars and bistros, avant-garde galleries and alternative theatres.

Photo: The Grand' Place and the Maison du Roi

Brussels is more than just cool. It's colourful and exuberant, full of fault lines and contradictions, but it's the quintessential 21st-century capital city. This is where the post-modern future is being shaped. Pioneering crossover experimentation is the driving force behind the rapidly growing creative industries. But initially Brussels will confuse. Belgium's capital is officially bi-lingual. The vast majority of its citizens speak French, but, many say, only between 6pm and 8am. Every day some 200,000 Flemings commute into the city. They speak Dutch, the language of non-francophone Belgium. Not heard quite so frequently but still ever-present are Arabic, Turkish and Congolese, the softer Spanish of Latin Americans or the coarser voices of eastern Europe and Japan. English will also be ever-present, but it is an English spoken with many different native and non-native accents. Over 30 percent of the city's total population of around 1.2 million are immigrants, many of them illegal; another 20 percent are 'new Belgians', i.e. the children of immigrants with Belgian passports.

A melting pot of migrants and diplomats

Sometimes the differences are stark. For example, when after Sunday mass at Notre-Dame de la Chapelle, Poles mingle with the long-established *brusseleir*-speaking locals in the mainly working-class Marolles quarter. But the various cultures generally rub along well together.

The appearance of the city is just as diverse. Old buildings get torn down, renovated and rebuilt, but don't expect any uniformity. Individualism Brussels-style demands that one is different from one's neighbour. So there's new next to old, high-rise beside low-rise and beautiful alongside shabby. The division into Upper Town and

A welcome gesture at the Schuman roundabout – behind the welcoming hostess, the glass palaces of the EU quarter

Lower Town also causes confusion. Each half has its own centre, each half has its own quartiers and each quartier its own distinctive atmosphere. The Upper Town is more Parisian in character, metropolitan, but with exotic pockets, such as the predominantly Congolese Matongé quarter.

The more down-to-earth Lower Town extends out from both sides of the canal. Once, when it was home to many poor immigrants, the waterway served as a demarcation line. But now it is less obvi-

> **All roads lead to the Grand' Place**

ous. Old factories and warehouses are mutating into art galleries, showrooms, music clubs and attic flats; dreary tenements are being transformed into chic apartments and office complexes. Pleasant walkways now run alongside the concrete walls of the canal, where yachts belonging to the rich and famous bob gently on the water. Some belong to the children of immigrants, who are slowly but surely climbing the social ladder. Many are now lawyers, doctors, college lecturers or university professors, some city councillors, deputies, portfolio holders or government ministers. Even the sometimes rather snobbish immigrés de luxe have recognised this. Although one corner of Laeken is home to the Belgian royal family, it is basically a working-class district and now it even has a European School! The interface used to be higher up, on the edge of the steep hill. At the top lived the aristocracy. The majestic site first attracted the dukes of Brabant, then the dukes of Burgundy, and finally came the court of Holy Roman Emperor Charles V and his Habsburg descendants. Below it lived the middle-class patricians and artisans.

This contrasting mix is nowadays called *brassage*. It's no accident the term derives from the brewery trade. The way to tell a true Bruxellois is by what he drinks. And it

won't be a pale pils beer. As well as the local *gueuze speciality*, which is sipped like champagne, the beer-drinking fraternity in Brussels love the strong abbey beers. A popular aperitif is half-en-half, a mixture of sparkling wine and white wine – neither are very popular on their own. Instead champagnes and burgundies in particular are drunk in large quantities – from Brouilly to Saint-Amour.

The magnificent Grand' Place, the Hôtel de Ville – the town hall – and splendid guild-houses testify to the power and prosperity of the town and its industrious citizens. In medieval times, they amassed fortunes from luxury goods, such as gold-brocaded tapestries and the finest lace. Given their wealth-creating status and growing self-confidence, they were quickly able to wrest far-reaching freedoms from their masters. All routes lead to the Grand' Place, its name accurately reflecting its status. Resplendent in the inner courtyard of the Hôtel de Ville is a star. It is from this point that the distances to the country's borders are measured. But even as you stand on the country's showpiece square, there are stark contrasts just around the corner. Just a few streets away, behind the 'world's finest theatre', according to the French writer Jean Cocteau, the doors of gambling dens, peep shows and sex bars are open for business. Clearly evident at the start and end of the grands boulevards laid out in Parisian Haussmann-style is the phenomenon known as 'Brusselisation'. This is what urban planners and sociologists throughout the world call the desecration of whole districts, a consequence of uncontrolled property speculation and corrupt politics. A mini-Manhattan emerged in the Quartier Nord. Towering above Bruxelles-Midi station, where the high-speed TGV, Thalys and Eurostar trains terminate, is a new business quarter. However, time has healed some wounds. The Quartier Nord now looks a lot prettier. Lessons have been learned from the sins of the past. Now, far more care is taken to ensure plans are sustainable.

Invented in Brussels: Art Nouveau

But joie de vivre and an openness to new ideas are also characteristics of the Bruxellois. Many are lured out for weekend strolls by the markets, which range from antique and flea to stalls selling local produce and organic food. They wander, gaze, handle, taste and on the way home sip an apéro or buy a delicious fruit tart to take back for tea with mother or for their own dessert. And as they saunter through the avenues, rues and boulevards, the city's architectural treasures are revealed. These include the countless Art Nouveau buildings. Not just patrician mansions, but schools, swimming pools, warehouses and shops. After all, not everyone realises that Brussels is the home of Art Nouveau. It suited the city's temperament. This was a place where freemasons and liberals, open-minded Jews and revolutionaries-in-exile entered into a symbiotic relationship. Then to this open-minded attitude add the wealth accumulated in the industrial heartlands of Wallonia and the Brussels banking community. A concern for their fellow man is another characteristic typical of Brussels folk. During the German occupation between 1940 and 1944, countless Jews, political refugees and resistance fighters found refuge and safety behind the many splendid facades.

This mentality has its background in Belgium's rather murky colonial history. The country's capital city owes its grandeur and open spaces to the Congo. King Leopold II acquired an empire on the equator at the end of the 19th century. Desperately needing new markets and new sources for raw materials, the profits accruing from the exploitation of this giant colony were invested in an extravagant expansion of Brussels. Examples of this largesse can be seen in the Triumphal Arch in the Parc du Cinquantenaire, in the palatial Musée Royal de l'Afrique Centrale in Tervuren, in splendid avenues and in spacious parks, where rich and poor, young and old can relax and unwind. Now heavy traffic roars along the avenues, while the parks attract the au pair girls, who care for the children of the city's elite, and matronly Moroccan mothers with a cluster of children in tow.

Brussels only really starts to come alive as day-light fades. That's when the bars and restaurants begin to fill up, catering for every taste, from the down-to-earth to huppé (fashionable), from the exotic to jeune cuisine. But true creativity is unfolding in the theatres and the jazz clubs, caf'

Cosmopolitan chic with a slightly ironic aloofness

conc and discos, converted market halls or sugar factories, even in the renowned, 300-year-old Théâtre Royal de la Monnaie and the world-famous Art Deco concert hall in the Palais des Beaux-Arts.

The multi-cultural mix brought new dance forms and expressive circus, fusions of Moroccan folklore and techno, modern jazz and south Indian sounds; Rwandan rhythms merged with those of the Dutch Antilles, Irish folk songs and eastern European voices. And, everything that spills out on to the street motivates an army of fashion designers, film-makers, installation artists, painters, writers, photographers and advertising folk,

The colours of Africa – many immigrants from the Congo live in the Matongé quarter

at the same time drawing in bohemians, students and young people. This vibrant cultural scene then tempts the locals, the young Flemings and Walloons, the Poles and the Irish, the people who have nothing whatsoever to do with the EU or Nato.

Brussels is no longer a city to escape from, but increasingly a place to move to. Trend-watchers say Brussels has taken over from Berlin and Barcelona as Europe's cultural hotspot. Visitors can also experience for themselves this cosmopolitan chic, if they adopt a typical Brussels mindset: the word is convivial, which here means someone who although phlegmatic, with a slightly ironic aloofness, is basically infinitely open-minded, exudes humanity and is boundlessly curious. A little idleness, a surge of initiative, a spirit of adventure, et voilà: a capital city with so many fascinating faces. Bienvenue! Welkom!

WHAT'S HOT

1 Love to shop

Love shops They are very tasteful, but also a bit naughty. Brussels boasts a number of upmarket sex shops for women in search of elegant underwear and exclusive skincare products. *Lady Paname*, for example, is more boudoir than boutique *(rue des Grands Carmes 5)*. At *Eva Luna* it's silk and velvet and not just on the shelves. The whole shop is fitted out with it *(rue du Bailli 41, photo)*. *Bella Donna* has also adapted itself to meet the sensuous needs of its customers *(boulevard Adolphe Max 125)*.

Nice & slow

2

Slow food It's taken a while for slow food *(www.karikol.be)* to break through in the home of french fries. It's slow food only at *Le Max (av. Emile Max 87, www.lemax.be)*, *Le Zinneke (place de la Patrie 26, www.lezinneke.be)* and *Orphyse Chaussette (rue Charles Hanssens 5)*. These restaurants also take part in tastings and talks at the annual slow food meeting *Goûter Bruxelles*.

Retro rides into the future

3

The E-Solex trumps the e-bike The 1940s hybrid VeloSolex was never a fashion item. But power-assisted bikes are back – and now with a green electric motor. You can hire an E-Solex (photo) at *Vélo-Cité (place Colignon 13–15, www.velocite.be)* and *Cycles Devos (av. de la Couronne 500, www.cyclesdevos.com)*. If you'd like to take one home with you, then pay a visit to *Eurobike*. This is the place to come if you want to buy an e-bike that occasionally needs a bit of muscle power *(chaussée D'Helmet 150, www.eurobike.be)*.

Designer dreams

Affordable accommodation Brussels boasts plenty of chic boutique hotels, but they are not cheap. However, visitors with a sense of style do not need to arrange a loan before spending a few days in the city. Bed and breakfasts such as *La Conciergerie* meet the very highest design expectations and it won't cost the earth; a Nespresso machine is even included in the room *(rue du Fossé-aux-Loups 32, www.laconciergerie.be)*. Supercool and centrally located, *La Casa BXL (rue Marché au Charbon 116, www.lacasabxl.com, photo)* exudes a hint of the Orient. If you don't mind paying a few euros more, you will love *Phileas Fogg*. Yes, it could be expensive, but that's because you won't want to check out *(rue Van Bemmel 6, www.phileasfogg.be)*. If budgets are really tight, then this hostel with ultra-modern furnishings and cool décor offers very good value for money *(2Go4, boulevard Jacqmain 99, www.2go4.be)*.

Wine instead of beer

For wine connoisseurs Brussels is deemed to be the city for beer, but that doesn't mean wine drinkers have to go without. On the contrary: wine bars are now very popular. That's no surprise, as there are so many fine bars à vins to choose from. *Les Dames Tartine (chaussée de Haecht 58)* has a cellar offering 300 wines and the food is excellent too. The ambience at *Oeno TK* is perfect for an intimate evening meal, the service is exquisite and the food always a winner *(rue Africaine 31, www.oenotk.be)*. It's bit more boisterous in *A Bout de Soufre*. This wine bar is usually packed with good-humoured imbibers, keen to try out the new arrivals on the wine list. The excellent food prepared by the chef, Arnold Dossou-Yovo *(rue Tasson-Snel 11, www.aboutdesoufre.com)*, is a bonus.

IN A NUTSHELL

BEER

In Brussels beer is not just simply beer. It is produced by the spontaneous fermentation of a particular type of wild yeast *dekkera bruxelliensis* (known also in brewing textbooks as *brettanomyces bruxelliensis* or *brettanomyces lambicus*) that is native to the valley of the River Senne and present in the air around Brussels. To get the best results barley malt, wheat malt and aged hops are mixed in shallow tanks at roof level during the cooler months from November to April. This is how the sour, cloudy lambic is made. It is left to mature in old oak barrels for up to three years. Beers of different vintages are blended and a secondary fermentation takes place in bulbous bottles. The result is the fresh, sparkling ● *gueuze*, which, because of the way it is made, is known affectionately, if slightly self-mockingly, by the locals as 'our champagne'. Sometimes cherries are fermented whole with lambic to make kriek. Other specialities use raspberries, peaches or grapes. In Brussels only the Cantillon family business produces gueuze and there are about a dozen microbreweries to the west in nearby Pajottenland. A real insider's tip is to try the speciality beers developed in recent years by a new generation of brewers, who are challenging the traditional Brussels' brewing dynasties, e.g. Ekla Super Pils by L'Imprimerie and La Saison, Stouterik and Zinnebir by Brasseries de la Senne.

Photo: Charleroi Canal, Quai des Charbonnages

Beer, bobos and the *bande dessinée* – the face of Brussels is constantly changing

BOBOS

Yuppies are out. Their unashamedly ostentatious consumerism is no longer in tune with the spirit of the times. The *bobos – bourgeois-bohémiens* or middle-class bohemians – have degrees and creative ideas, and earn as much as the yuppies, but they are more discreet. No souped-up luxury cars, conspicuous designer clothes and home cinemas in wickedly expensive apartments, but pretty, renovated houses in gentrified Saint-Gilles or Ixelles. They enjoy a full cultural life with avant-garde tendencies – they are in a class of their own.

CHANSONS

Few people realise that Brussels is a citadel of the chanson – a song yes, but one that follows the rhythms of the French language. The famous chanson-nier, Jacques Brel (1929–78), was a true blood ketje as they call their children in these parts. He spent the latter years of his life in Tahiti, yet retained his primary residence in his home town until

The freemasons' legacy – an exhibition on the art of Chinese healing at the ULB's Museum of Medicine

his death. He is remembered for his hit Bruxelles in which he sings the praises of a town destroyed. In *Madeleine* he lavishly praises the local French fries, while in Les bonbons he glorifies the Grand' Place and pralines. A contemporary and close friend of Brel, Barbara, also began her career in the same Brussels clubs. The cosmopolitan nature of today's Brussels is inspiring chansonniers, such as the Belgians Arno, Maurane and Marie Warnant. One really hot tip: Marie Daulne and her girls from Zap, Mama and Baloji, Belgians of Congolese descent, who are putting the Brussels' Matongé quarter on the map.

CIRCUS

The EU's circus is a frequent source of mockery, especially in reference to the European Parliament's carousel rotating between Brussels, Luxembourg and Strasbourg. Paradoxically, Brussels is circus city. Known in French as les arts circassiens, new forms of expression, borrowed mainly from film, performance art, dance and the theatre, are being showcased to hundreds of children and young people at the *École de Cirque de Bruxelles*. This school has been in existence for nearly 30 years and there are currently over 600 students on the roll. It is very proud of its special programmes developed for those with learning difficulties. Many of the gifted students and brilliant teachers at the *École Supérieure des Arts du Cirque* or ESAC have come from all over the world as this college ranks among the best of its kind. Here they forgo animal training and clowns and instead focus on acrobatics and expressive dance. The students regularly display their talents in the college's magnificent Art Nouveau hall, in the *Halles de Schaerbeek* or in the *Espace Catastrophe,* which together with the *Maison du Cirque,* an association for the promotion and development of the circus arts, is probably the most important springboard for a career in the circus. Find more out about the circus in Brussels at *www. lamaisonducirque.be.*

COMICS

Brussels is the true ● home of the comic. In 1929 Georges Remi (otherwise known universally as Hergé), a native of Brussels, published his first tale about Tintin and Milou (or Snowy as the dog later became in English-language versions). His style of drawing, known as ligne claire (clear line) was instrumental in the development of Brussels – then as now an important centre for journalism and publishing – as a magnet for the creative brains behind what has been termed the 'ninth art'. Before long other Brussels comic artists were conquering the world: André Franquin with his fictional animal, Marsupilami, and Edgar P. Jacobs with Blake and Mortimer. The most successful of all were to be Peyo's Smurfs. In the 1980s the leading lights were Philippe Geluck, the inventor of Le Chat, the precocious cat, François Schuiten (Fantastic Cities) and Yslaire (The 20th Sky). Among the younger generation of comic artists, the most important include Dominique Goblet, Midam and Thierry van Hasselt. The Centre Belge de la Bande Dessinée (Belgian Comic Strip Centre) offers a fascinating overview. There's also the city's unique Comic Strip Route. In 1991 a decision was made to commemorate the most popular fictional characters, while masking the gable ends of some otherwise rather shabby terraces. Now almost 40 walls have been covered in massive tributes to 35 or so Belgian comic strip artists.

THE CONGO

While still a young man, the future king Leopold II had one clear objective: he wanted Belgium to have a colony too. He thought Europe's second economic power needed a show of grandeur, but he also wanted new markets, possibly for the country's railway engineers, and also new sources of raw materials. The Berlin Conference of 1884–85, which divided Africa among the colonial powers, awarded Belgium the 'heart' of the continent. He declared it to be his own private property. The opening up of the huge Congo Free State swallowed up vast sums of money. The king was forced to borrow from the government and mortgage the Congo. In 1908 it passed into the ownership of the Belgian government. This vast private royal domain did, however, yield considerable benefits. It supplied rubber for the booming tyre industry. The labourers suffered brutal treatment and many lost their lives, for which Leopold II suffered international condemnation. He was caught in a dilemma: on the one hand he was against the maltreatment of the Congolese work force, yet, at the same time, he was eager for the proceeds from it.

The profits were spent on, amongst other things, government buildings and the redevelopment of the Belgian capital. His Royal Palace was given an imperial makeover, and the private residence Château de Laeken gained imposing side wings and magnificent royal greenhouses. Works by celebrated sculptors found their way into the Parc du Cinquantenaire, as did an impressive Triumphal Arch. During the expansion of the city the king insisted on the construction of long, Parisian-style boulevards. In the new districts he purchased vast tracts of land via agents in order to develop landscaped parks. Today these assets contribute to Brussels' quality of life as well as to the well-being of the Congolese and other Africans, who emigrated to the Belgian capital in post-colonial times to escape ethnic conflicts and economic hardship under the new dictatorships.

ENVIRONMENT

In 1980 the Green party Ecolo was founded in francophone Belgium. Since then it has steadily grown in influence. In the years between 1995 and 2006, the Greens provided the portfolio holders responsible for urban and regional planning in the municipality of greater Brussels, and, since 2004, there has been a Green minister for the environment in the Brussels Regional Government. In the regional elections of 2009 Ecolo received a very respectable 20 percent of the vote. The other parties have gradually been adopting the Greens' philosophy, to the benefit of the residents. They are encouraging cycling and the use of public transport, and are planting increasing numbers of trees along the streets.

Parts of the green belt are under environmental protection thus safeguarding biodiversity. More and more of the urban districts are also providing sites for organic allotments. If planning permission procedures take too long the Green Guerilla will plant flowers and shrubs at the dead of night – illegally of course – but this is tolerated with typical Brussels sang-froid. That tolerance ends, however, when Green activists let the air out of the tyres of gas-guzzling 4x4 vehicles.

FASHION

It is thanks to the La Cambre École Supérieure des Arts Visuels and the École Supérieure des Arts Saint-Luc and, most of all, to the public relations success of the fashion show *Modo Brussels* and its awards, that the stars of the Brussels fashion scene are conquering the world. José Enrique Oña Selfa is creative designer of haute couture for Loewe. Jean-Paul Knott is calling the tune not only in his own Brussels house but also at Cerrutti, and his long-time assistant Cédric Charlier is doing likewise at Cacharel. Olivier Theyskens moved from the upper echelons of Rochas via Nina Ricci to the New York cult brand Theory. Laetitia Crahay is Head of Accessory Design at Chanel. Xavier Delcour is the darling of rock and pop, from Mick Jagger to Placebo. Daniele Controversio is a designer with the cult brands Diesel, La Maison Margiela and Vivienne Westwood. Cathy Pill and Gérald Wathelet are running successful fashion houses in Paris, whilst Christophe Coppens with his avant-garde accessories is an important player on the global stage.

FREEMASONS

The freemasons of Brussels have left their mark with a unique symbiosis of science and economics, politics and art. In 1834 the lodges founded the Université Libre de Bruxelles (ULB) to counter the growing influence of the Catholic University of Leuven. All research and teaching there was subject to strict papal dogma, whereas the ULB chose as its motto Scientia vincit tenebras (Science conquers darkness), thereby casting off the doctrinal straitjackets. As a result, great progress was made in the field of medicine, and new disciplines, such as sociology and commerce, were introduced.

In 1846 a group of freemasons who had studied at the ULB – in particular those who had taken law – founded the Liberal Party. Their policies were advanced in the lodges; in effect the entire political elite was educated at the ULB. Up to 1983 the Liberal Party provided every single mayor of Brussels. Then for the first time a socialist moved into the Hôtel de Ville in the Grand' Place, but he, too, was a Mason. So once again it was the more progressive brethren from the lodge who were shaping the political landscape. They had founded the Belgian Workers' party in 1885.

However, as well as the political and scientific legacy, art, too, was heavily influenced by the freemasons. Victor Horta (1861–1947), the artistic genius behind Art Nouveau, was a freemason. His first work was a villa for the academic staff at the ULB. The innovative central staircases with landings opening seamlessly into the rooms, and glass domes up above to let in light were examples of the pioneering spirit within freemasonry. The connection between the lodges and the world of politics resulted in Victor Horta and his staff receiving many public commissions. Schools and swimming baths, housing estates and hospitals, the Palais des Beaux-Arts and the Central Station are all proof of just how the Art Nouveau movement shaped the city's civic fabric. Although not always quite so evident, freemasons still have considerable influence at Free University of Brussels.

PROTESTS

Belgians and especially the Bruxellois are inveterate *rouspeteurs*, i.e. whingers and troublemakers. No wonder, then, that they enjoy an argument and a demonstration. Barely a week passes without a protest march. Animal rights activists and idealists, pilots and police voice their concerns with banners and megaphones and by marching down the boulevards or staging sit-ins. They are allowed to assemble anywhere except outside the Parliament and the Royal Palace. Protests in the European Quarter are usually more colourful and boisterous. Groups from all over Europe, from Lapland to Gibraltar, regularly assemble outside the EU Commission and the Council of Ministers to rail against an upcoming directive.

RETURN TO THE CITY

Like all big cities, Brussels has been

Bicycles for hire at 180 locations in Brussels

blighted by the exodus of its better-off families from the urban quarters to the leafy suburbs. Since the middle of the 1990s, however, the number of inner-city dwellers has once again been on the increase. Highly-qualified young people on good salaries, some with children, are returning to the city. Little by little they are displacing the poorer social groups in districts that still have the charm of the Belle Époque. Attic flats in former factories and warehouses are in demand, as are high-rise apartments, the higher the better. Not pretty from down below, but with a glorious view.

THE PERFECT DAY
Brussels in 24 hours

08:00am ALONE ON THE GRAND' PLACE

Start the day here and you will get the 'finest theatre in the world' all to yourself. Early in the morning only a few folk are out and about on the *Grand' Place* → p. 29, so this is the time to study in peace the countless details of the magnificent Hôtel de Ville and the ornate guildhouses, both symbols of the wealth amassed by the burghers of Brussels during the Middle Ages.

09:00am DIVINE SPLENDOUR

First of all sit down on one of the benches in the grassy area in front of the *Cathedral* → p. 34 and then marvel at the harmonious proportions and the delicate ornamentation on the exterior of this fine building (photo left). Now you can go in. Just stand still and admire the majestic stained-glass windows, the Baroque statues on the columns and the huge, carved pulpit.

10:00am ROYAL SPLENDOUR

Now look out over the Lower Town: from the place Royale with its symmetrically aligned, whitewashed palais, the view encompasses the Palais de Justice, the Church of Sainte-Marie at the end of rue Royale and the Parc de Bruxelles with the Palais du Roi. Visible in the distance are the glittering spheres of the Atomium. But now would be the perfect time for a coffee break and the cafeteria in the *Musée des Instruments de Musique* → p. 37 is the ideal spot. Its sun terrace affords a magnificent panoramic view.

11:00am SURREALIST ART

Now it's time for some art appreciation. In subtly illuminated rooms the *Magritte Museum* → p. 38 showcases masterpieces and documents from the life of the Belgian surrealist painter, René Magritte (photo right).

12:00pm TREATS FOR THE EYES AND THE TASTE BUDS

Brussels' smart set meets on the pretty *place du Sablon* → p. 41. If you would like to observe the little game of 'see and being seen', ideally you should find a seat in the Au *Vieux Saint-Martin*, a popular meeting place for young and old, with the added bonus that there is a wide range of delicious local specialities on the menu. Follow this with a visit to *Marcolini* → p. 73 where you can buy melt-in-the-mouth chocolate creations.

Discover the best that Brussels has to offer – in the heart of the city, stress-free and all in a day

02:00pm ART NOUVEAU PERFECTION

Pay a visit to the *Musée Horta* → p. 47 and it will feel as if you are a personal guest of Victor Horta himself – even if he's not there to open the door. Horta built his own house when he was at the pinnacle of his career, ensuring every detail met his stringent design criteria.

03:00pm A RICH MIX

Now it's time to enjoy the here and now. The area around the attractive *Étangs d'Ixelles* → p. 46 and the décor in the arty *Belga café* → p. 76 encapsulate the special charm of Brussels. This is the part of town where you will encounter women parading the streets with lap dogs, Filipino au pairs, silent anglers and students from the nearby fashion academy in avant-garde gear.

05:00pm AT EUROPE'S CONTROL CENTRE

Rond-Point Schuman provides a good platform from which to survey the EU's glass palaces. The European Commission is based in the star-shaped building known as *Berlaymont* → p. 43. To the left of the roundabout, the *Council of Ministers* → p. 95 wields power from a pinkish-grey office block. While in the background the *Triumphal Arch* in the Parc du Cinquantenaire → p. 44 recalls Belgium's colonial past.

06:00pm HAPPY HOUR

If when it comes round to happy hour time you feel like an aperitif, you are sure to encounter many like-minded Bruxellois. They will be sitting in the fashionable bars around *place Saint-Géry* → p. 32 enjoying a Belgian beer or a cocktail. At the weekend *L'Archiduc* → p. 75 resounds to live jazz (photo).

08:00pm CONCERT & FINE DINING

It could be music, dance or theatre, but whatever is on, a performance in the magnificent Art Deco *Palais des Beaux-Arts* → p. 80 will prove to be a memorable experience. After that you can see out the day in style in *Kwint* → p. 62 over truffles and caviar.

Metro for the starting point: Lines 3, 4
Station: Bourse
Purchase a day ticket for only 4.50 euros and you can go almost everywhere – a single ticket costs 1.80 euros

SIGHTSEEING

CITY WHERE TO START?

Grand' Place (125 E4) (☐ G3):
The main square makes an ideal starting point for (first-time) visitors. Walk for a few minutes and you will find yourself in the elegant, 19th-century Galeries Saint-Hubert shopping arcade and the fashionable rue Antoine Dansaert. A short walk through gardens leads to the cathedral, to museums and cafés. There are large, well-signposted, underground car-parks near the Grand' Place and place de La Monnaie. Metro stations: Bourse (3, 4) and Gare Centrale (1, 5), trams 92 and 94 stop near the museums (Royale).

The contrasts that make Brussels such a lively city are evident not just in the urban landscape but also in the many museums, where precious artefacts and objets' d'art abound.

It is a city visited by fine art enthusiasts wishing to admire works by giants from the world of painting, such as Bosch, Bruegel, Rubens, Van Dyck and Magritte, but many also come to marvel at treasures from antiquity or keep up-to-date with the latest trends in contemporary art. Others come simply to explore the city's long and distinguished past and some come for … comic strips. When planning your visit it is worth bearing in mind that most museums are closed on Monday. So why did Brussels become the home for

Photo: Place Royale

A city of contrasts – Art Nouveau and medieval prosperity, narrow lanes and fashionable squares, design and diplomacy

this vast collection? It is in part thanks to the wealth accumulated by its merchants over the centuries, its favourable location at the intersection of important trade routes being an important factor here, but also because the city fathers have always been fascinated by art and culture. It started with the patrician dynasties of the late 10th century, there were the dukes of Burgundy and Holy Roman Emperor Charles V, then came Prince Charles Alexandra of Lorraine, who employed only the best artists at his court. During the 19th century, a new liberal elite of industrialists and bankers enticed Europe's avant-garde to the city. And then in 1893, Art Nouveau or 'new art' took root here. This movement that transformed the world of the decorative arts and architecture swept away traditional, classical-style concepts and laid the foundations for Art Deco and Surrealism. In 1958, the year of the first World Fair or Expo since World War II, the new emerging powers in Europe, known then as the European Economic Community,

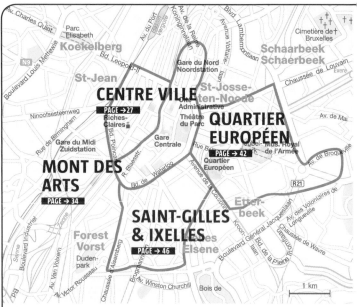

The map shows the location of the most interesting districts. There is a detailed map of each district on which each of the sights described is numbered.

chose to establish their headquarters in the Quartier Européen or EU Quarter, triggering a building boom that continues to this day.

CENTRE VILLE

The city's heart is the splendid Grand' Place and its main arteries are the wide boulevards, which radiate from the central zone. Within a stone's throw of each other are the Hôtel de Ville, Brussels' town hall, the Bourse (stock exchange), the Théâtre de la Monnaie opera house, plus many other theatres and cinemas. Around the smart rue Antoine Dansaert live fashion designers, film-makers and young EU officials, in the adjoining streets immigrants from all corners of the globe.

1 BOURSE (125 E3) (ⓜ F3)

In the middle of the 19th century, the city fathers decided to modernise the Old Town. Taking Paris as its model, grands boulevards were built between the northern and southern railway stations. The new stock exchange was to be an important landmark. The friezes and sculptures adorning this splendid building symbolise Belgium and its diverse industrial sectors. The allegorical figures representing Asia and Africa on the corners of the western side are the work of Auguste Rodin. *Place de la Bourse | metro: Bourse*

2 CENTRE BELGE DE LA BANDE DESSINÉE ★ ● (125 F3) (ⓜ G2)

Tintin and Snowy, Lucky Luke and the Smurfs: all are popular comic-strip heroes with leading roles at the Belgian Comic Strip Centre. The permanent collection documents in chronological order the development of the genre, while changing exhibitions look more closely at the classic and avant-garde examples of the art form. It was Victor Horta, the inspirational figure behind Art Nouveau, who between 1903 and 1906 created this magnificent structure with its striking glass ceilings. It was originally built for a textile wholesaler. Many devotees of the comic strip come to the Comic Centre to browse the world's largest specialist library in the world (approx. 40,000 volumes) and also to take advantage of the excellent book and souvenir shop. *Tue–Sun 10am–6pm | admission 8 euros | rue des Sables 20 | www.cbbd.be | metro: 1, 5: Gare Centrale*

■3■ EDITIONS JACQUES BREL
(125 E4) (*ᗰ G3*)

The famous chansonnier was born in Brussels in 1929. He made his début in small cabarets and, despite spending much of his later career in Paris, for the whole of his life he retained his family home here in the city centre. Brel's widow, Miche, and his daughter, France Brel, stage regular exhibitions to showcase aspects of the life and work of a singer remembered chiefly for the intensity of his lyrics and an unmistakeable voice. *Sept–June Tue–Sun noon–6pm, July/Aug daily 10am–6pm | admission 8 euros | place de la Vieille Halle aux Blés 11 | www. jacquesbrel.be | metro 1, 5: Gare Centrale*

■4■ GALERIES SAINT-HUBERT ●
(125 E3) (*ᗰ G3*)

Karl Marx cursed the 'ugly face of capitalism' during the building work, for a working class district had to be demolished to make way for this temple dedicated to consumerism and indulgence. This magnificent neoclassical shopping arcade with an extravagant glass roof houses luxury shops, restaurants, cinemas and a theatre – above them many fine apart-

---

ments. René Magritte painted the ceiling in the *Théâtre Royal des Galeries*. *Rue des Bouchers | metro 1, 5: Gare Centrale*

■5 GRAND' PLACE ★ (125 E4) (*⌖ G3*)

This is where the city comes alive. Locals, new arrivals, visitors, newly-weds and state visitors mingle on the cobbles of what was described by Jean Cocteau as 'the finest theatre in the world'. And the terraces in front of the bars and restaurants form its boxes. Young people enjoy the relaxing atmosphere on the steps up

Grand' Place – the beating heart of Brussels

to the *Maison du Roi*. Only from there does the full grandeur and elegance of the *Hôtel de Ville* become apparent | *Tue–Wed 2.30pm–4pm, Sun 10am–12.15 pm | admission 3 euros*). As if by a miracle, this symbol of the power of the bourgeoisie was one of the few buildings to survive the bombardment of Brussels by Louis XIV's army in 1695. The 91m-high (300ft) tower, topped by a gilt-metal statue of St Michael, the city's patron saint, asymmetrically breaks up the ornately-sculptured, late-Gothic facade. What used to be the Cloth Hall in the southwest corner of the inner courtyard was destroyed, but rebuilt in 1706 in strict Baroque style. This is where Brussels' mayors reside and decide. At the other corner, the city council assembles in a grand chamber. The self-confident burghers decorated it, as an emperor or a pope might, with fine tapestries and a ceiling fresco glorifying Brussels and Brabant.

After 1695, the city's guilds rebuilt their grand houses on the Grand' Place in record time, making sure they were even finer than before. Each one bears a special name. The unified, harmonious facade of what is called the Maison des Ducs de Brabant – after the nineteen busts of the dukes of Brabant that adorn the facade's pillars – dominates the square. On the corner of the narrow rue au Beurre stands the Roi d'Espagne with its elaborate dome, once the seat of the bakers' guild. *L'Arbre d'Or* or Golden Tree at no.10 is the only guildhouse still owned by a guild, the Union of Belgian Brewers. Today it houses a Brewery Museum, where visitors are invited to sample some of Belgium's finest beers. *Metro:* Bourse

■6 ILOT SACRÉ (125 E3) (*⌖ G3*)

Even in the 1950s, the little lanes around rue des Bouchers and rue des Dominicains

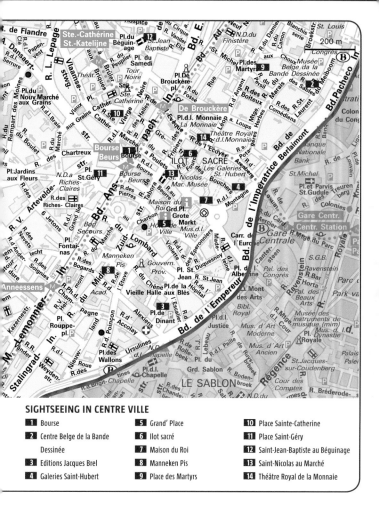

SIGHTSEEING IN CENTRE VILLE

1 Bourse

2 Centre Belge de la Bande Dessinée

3 Editions Jacques Brel

4 Galeries Saint-Hubert

5 Grand' Place

6 Ilot sacré

7 Maison du Roi

8 Manneken Pis

9 Place des Martyrs

10 Place Sainte-Catherine

11 Place Saint-Géry

12 Saint-Jean-Baptiste au Béguinage

13 Saint-Nicolas au Marché

14 Théâtre Royal de la Monnaie

---

were renowned for their variety theatres and bars where drinkers could enjoy live music. Jacques Brel, Georges Moustaki and Toots Thielemans all launched their careers there. Today, in this 'sacred' district, restaurants are forever seeking to outdo their competitors with tempting displays. Outside many of them tourists are pressured by persuasive touts and of-

ten end up paying inflated prices. Metro: *De Brouckère*

7 MAISON DU ROI (125 E4) (*G3*)
The magnificent rooms in the Museum of the City of Brussels house countless fascinating treasures. On display in the ground floor are some exquisite luxury goods, such as carved and painted

Manneken Pis – a symbol of the Bruxellois' contempt for authority

altarpieces, tapestries, porcelain and silver. The first floor explores the history of this powerful metropolis. Models, plans, paintings, prints and documents illustrate the stages of the city's development. *Tue–Sun 10am–5pm | admission 3 euros | Grand' Place | www.cbbd.be | metro: Bourse*

⑧ MANNEKEN PIS ●
(125 E4) (*m* F3)

Many legends surround the carefree urinating urchin, who has become something of a mascot for the city. Whatever one's views about its propriety, the masterful Baroque bronze perfectly expresses the Bruxellois' contempt for authority and need to poke fun. And it is precisely for this reason that the little Manneken Pis has been kidnapped on a number of occasions. Visitors to Maison du Roi (see

above) are always amused by the section exhibiting costumes and uniforms often jokingly donated to the city by foreign dignitaries to cover the Mannekin Pis' intimate parts. *Corner rue du Chêne/rue de l'Etuve | metro: Bourse*

⑨ PLACE DES MARTYRS
(125 F2) (*m* G2)

Beneath the Patria monument lie the bones of the more than 450 heroes, who saw off the Dutch occupiers in 1830. A little further on Henry van de Velde erected an Art Nouveau memorial to their leader, Louis-Frédéric de Mèrode. It dates from 1897. The square, ringed by classical buildings, is itself a monument to conservationists. Metro: De Brouckère

⑩ PLACE SAINTE-CATHERINE
(125 D–E3) (*m* F2)

A bright and cheerful market in front of a rather gloomy neo-Gothic church by Joseph Poelaert. This point marks the start of the fishmongers' quarter and fittingly a cluster of fish restaurants. *Metro 1, 5: Sainte-Catherine*

⑪ PLACE SAINT-GÉRY
(125 D3) (*m* F3)

There is a rapid turnover in property ownership around the old market hall. Young people from the world of film and TV, fashion and advertising, design and pop music are gradually taking over from the native population and recent immigrants. If it's cool, it's here. *Mappa Mundo is aspiring*, *Le Roi des Belges* opposite is the epitome of radical chic, slightly more alternative on the other hand is the *Zebra Bar* and the *Café des Halles* in the hall and on the terrace outside. In order to stimulate a debate about new ideas, the provincial government's Ministry for Conservation, Urban Planning, Social and Environmental Policies frequently organises interesting INSIDER TIP exhibitions on the first floor *(daily 10am–18pm | admission free | www.hallessaintgery.be | Metro: Bourse)*.

12 SAINT-JEAN-BAPTISTE AU BÉGUINAGE (125 E2) *(ø F–G2)*

Regarded as one of the finest Baroque buildings in Belgium, the church belonging to the former Beguine convent boasts a beautifully-structured facade, a lavishly-carved pulpit and confessionals, plus a number of valuable paintings. *Place du Béguinage | metro 1, 5: Sainte-Catherine*

13 SAINT-NICOLAS AU MARCHÉ (125 E3) *(ø G3)*

Shops and dwellings cling to the strangely lopsided church like dolls' houses. Saint-Nicolas au Marché is a fine example of how in earlier times the high cost of land led to innovative solutions. The church lay in one of the city's busiest quarters. In 1695 merchants funded its reconstruction in Baroque style, together with a gilded wrought-iron grille in front of the chancel and a painting by Rubens. *Rue au Beurre 1 | metro: Bourse*

14 THÉÂTRE ROYAL DE LA MONNAIE (125 E3) *(ø G2)*

Brussels' oldest temple to the Muses dates from 1695 and occupies the site of the old mint, hence the name. The architect of the Palais de Justice, Joseph Poelaert, designed the neo-Baroque interior after a fire. In 1985 post-modern rehearsal rooms were added. It's worth stepping inside to admire the foyer and the impressive Salon Royal, which were given a decorative makeover by modern artists Daniel Buren, Sam Francis, Sol LeWitt and Giulio Paolini. INSIDER TIP Superb chamber music concerts given by members of the orchestra in the majestic Grand Foyer *(Fri 12.30pm | admission 7.50 euros)*. The shop here is first-class *(Sept–June Tue–Sa t 11.30am–6pm and before and after performances)*. But it is chiefly the performances of opera, music concerts, ballet and dance that give this theatre its world-class reputation. *Guided tours: Sat noon | 8 euros | tel. 0 22 29 13 72 | www.lamonnaie.be | place de la Monnaie | metro: De Brouckère*

Place Saint-Géry – no dress code required

MONT DES ARTS

The slope between the Upper and Lower Town, between the cathedral and the Palais de Justice, was once the part of the city favoured by the nobility.

■■ **CATHÉDRALE SAINT-MICHEL** ★ ●
(125 F3) (*G–H3*)

The now superbly restored cathedral with its two square towers dominates the gentle slope. On the outside Gothic with typical Brabant lace embellishments around the portals, windows and battlements. On the inside numerous typically Renaissance and Baroque features stand

Cathédrale Saint-Michel – superbly-restored, with stained-glass windows and carvings

Now the Palais Royal, the Palais de la Nation and many of the ministries, the elegant *place Royale* and several respected museums surround the equally elegant Parc de Bruxelles. Upmarket antiques shops and smart cafés line the pavements around the place du Sablon, now a highly desirable spot for the well-heeled burghers of Brussels, whereas the Marolles quarter has remained fairly down-to-earth.

out. Most of the very fine stained-glass windows have survived the ravages of war. A 'Last Judgement' by Frans De Vriendt hangs proudly above the main double doors. In the nave lie Emperor Charles V and his wife Isabella of Portugal (north side) and his sister Marie with her husband King Louis II of Hungary (south side).

Behind the chancel, the Renaissance alabaster altar deserves more than a fleeting look, likewise the pulpit. Among the highlights from the Brussels school of woodcarving is the Baroque portrayal of Adam and Eve's Expulsion from Garden of Eden and the Legend of the Vine Leaf. Beneath the nave are remnants of a much older Romanesque church, beneath the chancel the graves of dukes of Brabant. Not only is it worth a look, but if you get the chance stop and listen to the INSIDER TIP 'swallow's nest' organ by Gerhard Grenzing. This imposing structure with no fewer than 4,300 pipes, 60 stops and four manuals was completed and solemnly blessed in 2000. *Parvis de Sainte-Gudule | www. cathedralestmichel.be | metro 1, 5: Gare Centrale*

2 JARDIN BOTANIQUE 🌿
(126 A–B2) (*ⅆ H2*)

From this quiet retreat you can appreciate the contrasting splendour of Brussels. On the right is the elegant, neoclassical greenhouse of the old Botanical Garden and surrounding parkland, on the left a towering office block, and below is the Quartier Nord, a glittering mini-Manhattan. In the distance the imposing Basilique Nationale du Sacré-Cœur Nationale closes off a long and impressive boulevard. In one direction the important cross-city axis, rue Royale, ends with the neo-Byzantine Church of Sainte-Marie, in the other with the Palais du Roi. This is one of the best places to be on a warm Brussels evening, as the setting sun is reflected in the greenhouse glass. *Admission free | corner bd du Jardin Botanique/rue Royale | metro 2, 6: Botanique*

3 LES MAROLLES
(125 D–E 5–6) (*ⅆ F4–5*)

There's a relic from the past residing in the social housing apartments (including a fine Art Nouveau block between rue de la Rasière and rue Pieremans):

THE BIRTHPLACE OF ART NOUVEAU

In 1893 Victor Horta (1861–1947) designed a house for Professor of Mathematics, Emile Tassel *(Hôtel Tassel, rue Paul-Emile Janson 6)*. Brussels was bowled over. Iron girders were left visible, wrought-iron railings twisted into flowers. Light poured in through huge windows and a glass dome. Rooms merged together off a central stairwell. Everything from door handles to taps was tailor-made. Also in 1893, Horta's colleague, Paul Hankar, went one step further with his own, equally daring residence *(rue Defacqz 71)*. L'Art nouveau or new art was born. And in an instant it had conquered the city – and soon after

the world. In 1897 the older Viennese architect, Otto Wagner, and the young Hector Guimard from Paris, came to the Brussels World Exhibition. They saw how Art Nouveau had taken off. But only in Brussels did it become a style adopted for the masses. Long before the term was officially coined in 1925, in Brussels Art Nouveau was evolving into Art Deco. Victor Horta was a pioneering force behind the movement, Joseph Hoffmann gave it a powerful impetus with *Palais Stoclet*. Around 1,500 flawless Art Nouveau buildings, and even more in Art Deco, have survived the wrecking ball of later generations.

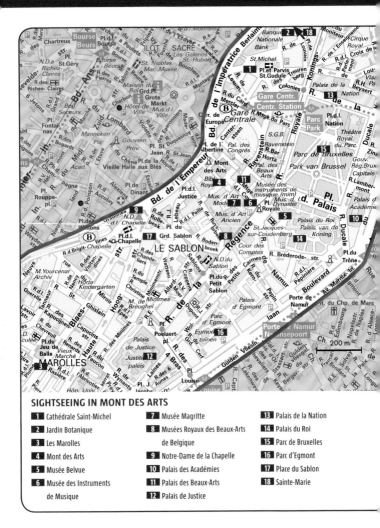

SIGHTSEEING IN MONT DES ARTS

- **1** Cathédrale Saint-Michel
- **2** Jardin Botanique
- **3** Les Marolles
- **4** Mont des Arts
- **5** Musée Belvue
- **6** Musée des Instruments de Musique
- **7** Musée Magritte
- **8** Musées Royaux des Beaux-Arts de Belgique
- **9** Notre-Dame de la Chapelle
- **10** Palais des Académies
- **11** Palais des Beaux-Arts
- **12** Palais de Justice
- **13** Palais de la Nation
- **14** Palais du Roi
- **15** Parc de Bruxelles
- **16** Parc d'Egmont
- **17** Place du Sablon
- **18** Sainte-Marie

he talks brusseleir (a mixture of Old Brabant and French), he whinges and whines, he drinks, he sings and he dances in the streets, but he is under threat from demographic change. Second-hand traders and better antique shops are getting ever closer to the flea market on the *place du Jeu de Balle* and smart new furniture shops and restaurants are opening up. The *Recyclart* café-restaurant *(rue des Ursulines 25)* is developing into a very popular haunt. Don't miss the restored *Horta kindergarten (rue Saint-Gislain 40)*. Metro 2, 6: Porte de Hal

4 MONT DES ARTS ❧
(126 A4) (🗺 G3)

The formal gardens designed by landscape architect René Pechère link the Upper Town and Lower Town in a most agreeable way. But there are also a number of important cultural institutions in the vicinity and so it's always a busy spot, in particular around the glass cube which serves as the entrance to the new Square Meeting Centre. Every 15 minutes, a cheery carillon rings out from the arch over rue Mont-des-Arts. In the ● *Librarium*, the *Bibliothèque Royale (www.kbr.be)* uses historic masterpieces and interactive computers to illustrate how the written word, the methods of publication and the gathering of knowledge has developed over five millennia *(Mon–Sat 9am–5pm | admission free). Place de l'Albertine/rue Mont-des-Arts/ rue Montagne de la Cour | metro 1, 5: Gare Centrale*

5 MUSÉE BELVUE
(126 A4) (🗺 H3–4)

A visit to the Belvue Museum is worthwhile for an interactive introduction (commentary in English) to the history of Belgium from 1830 to the present day, all documented in detail in a wing of the Palais du Roi complex. Remains of the Imperial Palace have been excavated from under the place Royale. In 1556 in the Aula Magna Charles V abdicated as ruler of the Holy Roman Empire and also as King of Spain. *Tue–Fri 10am–5pm, Sat–Sun 10am–6pm | admission 5 euros, combi-ticket to include museum and excavations 8 euros | place des Palais 7 | www.belvue.be | tram 92, 94: Palais*

6 MUSÉE DES INSTRUMENTS DE MUSIQUE ❧ (126 A5) (🗺 G3)

The words Old England look proudly out from the upper facade of this ornate, gracefully structured Art Nouveau building. Formerly a department store of the same name dating from 1899, this was where Brussels high society used to come shopping. At one time the leafy upper floor used to be the place for afternoon tea. But then the musical instrument museum moved in, although the café with sun terrace overlooking the place Royale continues to be a popular meeting place. On display here are instruments from all corners of the world, including a painted cembali and a bizarrely shaped

View of the Town Hall and Lower Town from the Mont des Arts

saxophone. The more robust instruments are often brought out for **INSIDER TIP** live performances. *Tue–Fri 9.30am–5pm, Sat–Sun 10am–5pm | admission 5 euros | rue Montagne de la Cour 2 | www.mim. be | metro 1, 5: Gare Centrale*

▉7▉ MUSÉE MAGRITTE ★
(126 A5) (*ᗅ G4*)

The classical white Altenloh Palais was completely refurbished for the opening

place Royale 1 | ticket sales: rue de la Régence 3, pre-purchase on the internet advisable | www.musee-magritte-museum. be | tram 92, 94: Royale

▉8▉ MUSÉES ROYAUX DES BEAUX-ARTS DE BELGIQUE
★ (126 A4) (*ᗅ G4*)

One day is hardly enough to see everything that this 200-year-old art museum has to offer. It is probably the paintings

Fantasy worlds – the laws of gravity don't apply in the Musée Magritte

of the museum in 2009. Its interior is illuminated in striking fashion and also decorated in blue and black, a colour combination that this painter of mysterious scenes loved. Displayed with hardly an empty space throughout the six-floors of this splendid building are around 200 outstanding pieces by René Magritte (1898–1967). From his very early attempts in fauvist style to later, world-renowned works, this collection showcases the life's work of the master of Surrealism. *Tue, Thu–Sun 10am–5pm, Wed 10am–8pm | admission 8 euros |*

by the Flemish primitives, Hieronymus Bosch and Hans Miemling, who attract most attention in the Royal Museums of Fine Arts of Belgium, to give it its English title. But Pieter Bruegel the Elder has two rooms to himself, gold-embroidered Brussels tapestries adorn the patio, and much space is devoted to works by Rubens, including many portraits. Also featured are paintings by one of Rubens' pupils, Anthony van Dyck, again including several portraits. Other highlights include the Dutch, e.g. Frans Hals and Rembrandt, and the French schools, e.g. Jacques-Louis David, Jean-Auguste-Dominiqe Ingres, to name but a few. Fine pieces by James Ensor, Fernand Khnopff and Edward Burne-Jones do justice to Brussels' role as a focal point for Symbolism. INSIDER TIP The museum café including a spacious terrace with views over the sculpture garden, is the perfect place to come when it's time for a break. Excellent chamber music concerts take place every Wednesday in the auditorium *(Oct–June 12.40pm)*. *Tue–Sun 10am–5pm (rooms are closed from to time because of staff shortages) | admission 8 euros, combi-ticket with the Magritte Museum 13 euros | rue de la Régence 3 | www.fine-arts-museum.be | tram 92, 94: Royale*

9 NOTRE-DAME DE LA CHAPELLE
(125 E5) (*Ø G4*)

A handsome Gothic church on the fringes of the Marolles quarter. At weekends it becomes the spiritual centre for Brussels' Polish community. A plaque in the fourth chapel on the right reminds visitors that the painter, Pieter Bruegel the Elder, and his wife, Marie Coecke, are buried here. *Place de la Chapelle | metro 1, 5: Gare Centrale*

10 PALAIS DES ACADÉMIES
(126 B5) (*Ø H4*)

This elegant building dates from the short Dutch period (1815–30). Originally built for Prince William of Orange in recognition of his much-acclaimed performance in the Battle of Waterloo, only later on the 19th century did the academies move in. The delightful gardens are not just a place for ageing scientists, writers and the élite from the arts world. *Rue Ducale 1 | metro 2, 6: Trône*

11 PALAIS DES BEAUX-ARTS ●
(126 A4) (*Ø G–H3*)

Victor Horta, the inspiration behind Art Nouveau, also pioneered elements of Art Deco, but the term did not enter the design world's vocabulary for another ten years. The Palais des Beaux-Arts, built between 1920 and 1928, perfectly illustrates Horta's mastery of architectural style. The large, oval-shaped concert hall, at the end of an audacious ramp, is underground. Galleries for exhibitions are clustered around a grand hall with a glass ceiling. The Palais, now usually

LOW BUDGET

▶ A magnificent view over the Old Town and the northern suburbs unfolds from the 🚇 ● square in front of the *Palais de Justice (125 E6) (Ø G4)*. A free lift will take you into the heart of the Marolles quarter, once a staunch working-class part of the city, but now slowly becoming gentrified.

▶ There is no admission charge for the *Musée Royale de l'Armée et d'Histoire Militaire (127 F5) (Ø L4) (Tue–Sun 9am–4.30pm)* – with a superb collection of arms and armoury. It's only a few yards from here to the 🚇 Triumphal Arch. It costs nothing to go up and there's a great view from the top.

▶ ● Many of Brussels' metro stations are decorated with fine works of art by celebrated Belgian artists, notably by Pierre Alechinsky (Anneessens), Paul Delvaux (Bourse) and Hergé (Stockel) – the underground network is almost a museum in its own right. A guide costing 5 euros is available from Porte de Namur and De Brouckère metro stations and also from the tourist offices.

referred to as Boar, also accommodates rooms for chamber music concerts, theatre and a cinematheque, where film classics are shown. Historians of English literature may be aware that the young Charlotte and Emily Brontë spent some time in Brussels as a plaque to the left of the entrance bears witness. *Guided tours Sunday at noon | price 7 euros | rue Ravenstein 23 | metro 1, 5: Gare Centrale*

🞮 PALAIS DE JUSTICE
(125 E6) (*∅ G4–5*)

The original inhabitants of the Marolles quarter use the term 'architect' as a term of abuse, their main target being Joseph Poelaert. To create the space for this huge building, much admired by Hitler and his architect Albert Speer, large sections of the Marolles quarter were cleared in 1866. Poelaert, who designed this monster and became insane before his death in 1879, glorified the concept of justitia and the might of Belgium. *Mon–Fri 9am–noon and 2pm–6pm | admission free | place Poelaert 1 | metro 2, 6: Louise*

🞮 PALAIS DE LA NATION
(126 B3–4) (*∅ H3*)

Belgium's two power bases symbolically face each other across the Parc de Brux-

elles: the Palais du Roi and the Palais de la Nation, Belgium's parliament building. One Belgian monarch once poked fun at the 'barracks' opposite. But the home of the Belgian Parliament, built in 1779 when Brussels was part of the Austrian Netherlands, is in no way inferior to the residence of the Belgian head of state. The committee rooms for the deputies and the Senate and also the galleries, where Belgian presidents meet their counterparts, are adorned in truly regal splendour. *Only by appointment (tel. 0 25 19 8111) and on 21 July | rue de la Loi | metro: Arts-Loi*

🞮 PALAIS DU ROI ★ ●
(126 A–B5) (*∅ H4*)

At one time the magnificent Imperial Palace, home to Burgundian and Habsburg kings, stood on this spot. But it was destroyed by fire in 1731 and was replaced by something much smaller. Leopold II had it converted into this still prestigious building. The interior exudes royal splendour, in particular the lavishly gilded Throne Room. In 2002 Belgium's Jan Fabre decorated the ceiling and lunettes in the Mirror Room with millions of glittering beetle carapaces. When foreign heads of state are visiting the Bel-

KEEP FIT!

Undulating woodland, known as *Bois de la Cambre* (130 C6) (*∅ J8*), is a favourite haunt of the jogging fraternity. Adjoining the park to the south is the 50 sq.km (20 sq.miles) *Forêt de Soignes* (tram 4, 94: Legrand). *Aspria Avenue Louise*, an upmarket fitness centre is a place where even James Bond would have been happy to work out. The

luxurious setting is the perfect place to get into shape. The ultra-sleek swimming pool is often used in advertising sequences and film backdrops. *Mon–Fri 6.30am–10pm, Sat/Sun 8am–8pm | guest ticket (for one day, massage included) 100 euros | (130 A2) (*∅ G5*) av. Louise 71B | tel. 0 25 42 46 66 | www. aspria.be | metro 2, 6: Louise*

Beetles in the Royal Palace – an insect installation by Jan Fabre in the Mirror Room

gian monarch, a frequent event, a guard regiment on horseback parades in front of the palace. *End July–early Sept (subject to when the king is in residence) daily 9.30am–4pm | admission free | place des Palais | metro 2, 6: Trône*

PARC DE BRUXELLES
(126 A–B4) (*ₘ H3*)

Brussels' oldest park both separates and connects the country's two power bases. The Prime Minister or President of the Senate regularly strolls through it for an audience with the king. Ambassadors and officials jog around it before lunch, two play areas give children space to let off steam and there are two cafés for a drink and a snack. The park was once part of the rulers' Imperial Palace, but in 1830 Belgian revolutionaries fought their way to independence from Holland here. Freemasonry has played an important role in Brussels' development and the layout of the park is testimony to their influence. *Rue Royale | metro 2, 6: Parc*

INSIDERTIP PARC D'EGMONT
(125 E–F6) (*ₘ G4*)

Four hidden gateways lead into this haven of tranquillity. English style contrasts starkly with the rear of the neo-Baroque *Palais d'Egmont*, the residence of the Belgian foreign minister. The Orangery houses an elegant café-restaurant with a shady terrace. It's a popular spot for a weekend brunch *(daily 9.30am–4.30pm)*. And it's a good starting point if you're interested in browsing through the wares of the antiques dealers on place du Grand Sablon or keen to explore the smart shops in the upmarket Porte Louise area. *Entrance near rue aux Laines 20 or on the left near the Hilton Hotel, bd. de Waterloo 38 | metro 2, 6: Louise*

PLACE DU SABLON ★
(125 E–F5) (*ₘ G4*)

A visit to this double square is an essential part of any visit to Brussels. The *Petit Sablon*, with its memorial to Counts Egmont and Horne, who paid with their lives for their rebellion against the Spanish, is ringed by small bronze statues. The *Grand Sablon*, on the other hand, is the focal point for antiques dealers; at weekends, it is the venue for their busy market. *Notre-Dame du Sablon*, a richly ornamented late-Gothic church, stands proudly between the two squares. Every evening, when the church is lit from within, the large stained-glass windows radiate a warm and cheerful light. Of special interest inside are the Renaissance galleries and the magnificent Baroque tombs of the princes of Thurn and Taxis, who ran the Imperial postal services throughout Europe during the Habsburg era. The Guild of Archers, who originally endowed the church, still stage their festivities here. *Tram 92, 94: Petit Sablon*

18 SAINTE-MARIE ☼
(126 B1) (*₥ H 1*)

Its copper dome and glittering gold mosaics clearly mark the end of rue Royale. This neo-Byzantine place of worship is now used as an ecumenical meeting place. Look out from the north side of the church and you will get a fine view of *Château de Laeken,* the royal residence. *Rue Royale | tram 92, 94: Sainte-Marie*

QUARTIER EUROPÉEN

● **Your first impression of the Quartier Européen is likely to be just another series of office blocks and a maze of urban expressways.**

But hidden away in between the office blocks are quiet parks, great museums and beautifully designed squares. Inhabiting the peripheral zones is a cosmopolitan mix of well-paid officials and lobbyists, clever interns learning their way around the EU's institutions and an army of poorer immigrants.

1 AUTOWORLD (127 F5) (*₥ L4*)

Fans of the internal combustion engine are irresistibly attracted to this stunning collection of some 500 gleaming limousines from the first Benz to the Cadillac Cabriolet, in which President Kennedy toured Berlin in 1963. Among the more unusual exhibits are some once very highly sought-after Belgian car marques, notably the Minerva. *April–Sept daily 10am–6pm, Oct–March daily 10am–5pm | admission 6 euros | Parc du Cinquantenaire 11 | www.autoworld.be | metro 1, 5: Mérode*

Autoworld – vintage and veteran vehicles are the stars behind the red carpet

2 AVENUE DE TERVUREN ☼
(O) (𝄞 M–O 4–5)

Despite the expressway, which was built in the 1960s over an elegant bridleway, and despite being lined by numerous soulless, functional buildings, this remains the finest road in the city. This grand avenue starts by the Triumphal Arch in the Parc du Cinquantenaire; it swings down from the Palais Stoclet to the lakes in the Woluwé valley and then climbs back up to the city forest. For the final stretch, it becomes a boulevard that goes on for several kilometres before reaching Musée Royal de l'Afrique Centrale. Beside this grand highway are numerous prestigious embassy buildings. *Metro 1: Montgomery*

3 BERLAYMONT ⏱
(127 D4) (𝄞 K3)

Stars symbolise the European Union. Which explains why the ground-plan for Berlaymont, the home of the European Commission, is star-shaped. When renovating the 1960s building, the Brussels architects, Steven Backers and Pierre Lallemand, looked for further symbolic parallels. The building is transparent and environmentally friendly. Only glass walls separate it from the road, mobile glass screens control light and heat in the offices. Recycled rainwater is used to flush the toilets and the exhaust air from the air-conditioning system heats the underground garage. *Rue de la Loi 200 | metro 1, 5: Schuman*

4 INSIDER TIP JARDIN JEAN-FÉLIX HAP (127 E6) (𝄞 K5)

There is nothing to disturb dreamers and courting couples in this romantic garden. It is a peaceful oasis of greenery with a pond fed by a bubbling spring. There's a small glazed pavilion, where visitors can shelter from a rain shower. *15 April–15 Oct*

Berlaymont, the EU's HQ – the site was formerly a convent

Mon–Sat 10am–noon and 2pm–6pm | chaussée de Wavre 512 | bus 34: De Theux

5 MAISON CAUCHIE (127 F6) (𝄞 L4)

It was not Victor Horta's floral lines, but Charles Rennie Macintosh's angular forms that influenced the painter, Paul Cauchie. He designed this house himself. Sgraffito, a fresco technique produced by applying layers of coloured plaster, covers a large part of the facade, which is adorned with nine muses. *First weekend of each month 10am–1pm and 2pm–5.30pm | admission 5 euros | rue des Francs 5 | www.cauchie.be | metro 1, 5: Mérode*

6 MUSÉE DES SCIENCES NATURELLES
(126–127 C–D6) (𝄞 J4)

The main attraction at the Museum of Natural Sciences is the vast collection of prehistoric remains, including the

10m-long (32ft) skeleton said to be 125 million years old. Interactive computers and the very latest audio-visual aids transport visitors back to a long-distant era. In the BiodiverCITY room, however, the theme is a modern one: how do flora, fauna and man cohabit in today's urban environment. Computers pose questions about personal decision-making and then simulate the consequence for biodiversity. Great cafeteria and shop. *Tue–Fri 9.30am–4.45pm, Sat/Sun 10am–6pm | admission 7 euros | rue Vautier 29 | www. sciencesnaturelles.be | bus 34, 80: Idalie*

Dinosaur skeleton in the Natural Science Museum

▨ MUSÉES ROYAUX D'ART ET D'HISTOIRE ★ ● ☀
(127 F5) (*Ø L4*)

With no fewer than 140 rooms, the Royal Museums of Art and History is one of the largest and most lavishly-stocked museums in the world (visitors please note that due to staff shortages and renovation work, some sections are either wholly or partially closed.) Displayed here are archaeological finds and works of art from four continents dating from prehistoric times to the 20th century. The most interesting rooms are those with artefacts from antiquity (e.g. a magnificent Roman mosaic excavated in what is now Syria), the Pre-Columbian cultures collection (Aztecs, Incas and Mayas), carved and decorated Belgian furniture from the Renaissance, Baroque and Rococo periods, famous Brussels tapestries (including some designed by Rubens) and carved, painted altarpieces, the Art Nouveau department with a number of stunning silver pieces (some by Henry van de Velde), some beautiful ceramics in mahogany display cabinets designed by Victor Horta for the Wolfers jewellery business and sedan chairs, coaches and carriages (for which Brussels was once famous). Delicious snacks are served in the cafeteria with terrace, from where there is a fine view over the Parc du Cinquantenaire. *Tue–Sun 10am–5pm | admission 5 euros | Parc du Cinquantenaire 10 | www. mrah.be | metro 1, 5: Schuman*

▨ PALAIS STOCLET (O) (*Ø N5*)

In 1905 Baron Adolphe Stoclet appointed the Viennese architect, Joseph Hoffmann, and in the city of floral Art Nouveau, he created a showpiece for the more geometric Vienna Secessionist movement. The exterior is finished entirely in marble and bronze and the huge mosaic frieze by Gustav Klimt in the dining room is often seen recreated in art history books. The house, still occupied by the Stoclet family, is never open to the public. To get a glimpse of this extravagant mansion, you will have to make do with a stroll along the fine Avenue de Tervuren. *Av. de Tervuren 275 | metro 1: Montgomery*

▨ PARC DU CINQUANTENAIRE ☀
(127 E–F5) (*Ø K–L3–4*)

Leopold II had this spacious green park laid out in 1880 to celebrate the 50th an-

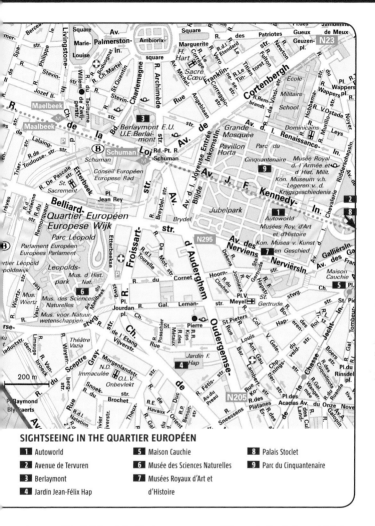

SIGHTSEEING IN THE QUARTIER EUROPÉEN

1 Autoworld
2 Avenue de Tervuren
3 Berlaymont
4 Jardin Jean-Félix Hap
5 Maison Cauchie
6 Musée des Sciences Naturelles
7 Musées Royaux d'Art et d'Histoire
8 Palais Stoclet
9 Parc du Cinquantenaire

niversary of the Belgian state. The imposing Triumphal Arch with its quadriga and semi-circular colonnade dominate the park. Only later did the Musées Royaux d'Art et d'Histoire, the Musée Royal de l'Armée et de l'Histoire Militaire and Autoworld move into the original, neoclassical exhibition halls. At the northeastern corner of the park stands Brussels' first and largest mosque. Alongside it the Temple of Human Passions, Victor Horta's first work. In fact, it is sometimes described as the Pavilion Horta. If you look through the keyhole, you can see the huge, sexually-explicit marble relief (1897) by Jef Lambeaux. *Metro 1, 5: Schuman, Mérode*

SAINT-GILLES & IXELLES

The middle classes, artists and students have always preferred this part of the city, where the grace and splendour of the Belle Époque have largely survived. It's worth taking a stroll here to admire the eclectic facades, beautiful Art Nouveau houses and idyllic squares and then maybe seek refreshment in one of the many fashionable watering holes.

1 AVENUE BRUGMANN ☆
(129 E5–6) (⌀ F–G 7–8)

This 4-km long (3 mi) boulevard with a fine vista and some splendid Patrician mansions showcases a textbook of architectural styles. Avenue Brugmann climbs gently and then drops steeply downhill. Initially in terms of architectural style historicism prevails. Designers looked to the past, choosing neo-Gothic, neo-Renaissance and neoclassicism (at no. 48 is the mansion that once belonged to the violin virtuoso Eugène Ysaye). But soon some magnificent examples of Art Nouveau appear: les Hiboux for example, after the owls in the gable (no. 53), the striking Hôtel Hannon on the corner of rue de la Jonction or a little further on (no. 80) the Hôtel Dubois with its huge lounge window – another piece by the master, Victor Horta. Behind no. 52 and accessible from the road is a magical garden by René Pechère As you descend, there follow masterpieces of Art Deco (Maison Haerens, no. 384) and of Henry van de Velde's Modernism (La Maison blanche, no. 421). Tram 92: Ma Campagne

2 ÉTANGS D'IXELLES (128 C3–5) (⌀ J6–7)
The city's finest promenade runs beside fountains, meadows and benches, passing two long, narrow lakes. Reflected in the water by place Flagey is a modernist building, formerly the home of the Maison de la Radio and unmistakably resembling the bow of a boat. One monument at the corner of the étang recalls Charles de Coster (1827–1879), author of the famous novel, The Legend of Thyl Ulenspiegel and Lamme Goedzak (1867), a 16th-century romance that enjoyed great popularity outside Belgium. The promenade ends at Abbaye de la Cambre. Style-oriented students from the École Nationale Supérieure des Arts Visuels de la Cambre have been bringing colour to this classical complex since 1928. Tram 81, bus 71: Flagey

3 INSIDER TIP HÔTEL HANNON
(129 E4) (⌀ G7)

This striking Art Nouveau house was built in 1902 by Jules Brunfaut for the engineer, world traveller and amateur photographer, Edouard Hannon. At its heart is an oval hall with a mosaic floor, an elegantly curving staircase and ornate, wrought-iron balusters. The large fresco on the wall recalls the myth of Orpheus and Eurydice. A circular conservatory with remarkable stained-glass windows – by Raphaël Evaldre, a pupil of Louis Comfort Tiffany – creates a twinkling light effect. The building, fully restored in 1980, is now home to l'Espace photographique Contretype, an organisation that preserves Hannon's oeuvre. Wed–Fri 11am–6pm, Sat/Sun 1pm–6pm | admission 2.50 euros | av. de la Jonction 1 | www.contretype.org | tram 92: Ma Campagne

4 INSIDER TIP LA LOGE
(130 B3) (⌀ H6)

The freemasons have left a lasting, positive legacy on Brussels. This former temple provides a fascinating insight into the progressive Le Droit Humain Masonic lodge. Changing architectural exhibitions held here. *Tue–Sun noon–6pm | admission 4 euros | rue de l'Ermitage 86 | www.aam.be | tram 94: Bailli*

Typical of Horta's concept is the central staircase, over which a double glass dome diffuses a gentle light. A revolutionary feature is the segmented column

Africa in Brussels – a mural in chaussée de Wavre in the Matongé quarter

5 MATONGÉ (130 B1) (*φ H4–5*)

The everyday life of Brussels' African community is played out in the triangle between chaussée d'Ixelles, chaussée de Wavre and rue de la Paix, although few of them actually live here. They come here for the brightly coloured fabrics, exotic fruit and restaurants, as well as vibrant African music, but it has little to offer the indigenous population. *Metro 2, 6: Porte de Namur*

6 MUSÉE HORTA ★ ●
(129 E4) (*φ G6*)

In 1898 Victor Horta, the famous Art Nouveau architect, built a home and a workshop for himself. He regarded it as his finest achievement. Striking throughout are the contorted, flame-like lines.

in the ground floor; it's actually a radiator. On the cramped, top floor, mirrors subtly convey a feeling of spaciousness. As always with Horta, the end result is a breathtaking work of art. *Tue–Sun 2pm–5.30 pm | admission 7 euros | rue Américaine 25 | www.hortamuseum.be | tram 92: Janson*

7 PLACE DU CHÂTELAIN ☼
(130 A4) (*φ H6*)

This square shaded in the summer by lines of linden trees is an idyllic spot with a rather provincial feel. But when the offices close, the cosmopolitan collection of beautiful people drift into the fashionable bars and cafés to take apéritifs. Others work out in the smart Golden Club, before they too join friends in the crowded pubs.

SIGHTSEEING IN SAINT-GILLES & IXELLES

1 Avenue Brugmann
2 Etangs d'Ixelles
3 Hôtel Hannon
4 La Loge

5 Matongé
6 Musée Horta
7 Place du Châtelain
8 Place Georges Brugmann

9 Porte de Hal
10 Saint-Gilles

The market on Wednesday afternoon is like a fashion parade. *Tram 94: Bailli*

8 INSIDER TIP PLACE GEORGES BRUGMANN ● (129 E5) (*U G8*)

A pretty park, lined with patrician Belle Époque houses, trendy restaurants and café terraces, the most popular of which being Gaudron, the perfect venue for Brussels' *bobos.* Another of their favourite haunts is *Winery* (no. 18), a wine bar with avant-garde décor. The *Librairie Candide* (no. 1) keeps the cosmopolitan crowd up-to-date, courtesy of its comprehensive collection of international newspapers. *Bus 60: Georges Brugmann*

9 PORTE DE HAL (129 D2) (*U F5*)

Where today cars race along the inner-city ring road, was once the old city wall. Sturdy gateways secured the most important access routes. The Porte de Hal, which dates from 1381, is the last remaining such portal. But this solid construction with a horseshoe-shaped ground-plan is more like a fortress. It convincingly conveys an impression of power and wealth. Inside, exhibits document the defence of the city over the centuries. *Tue–Fri 9.30am–5pm, Sat/Sun 10am–5pm | admission 5 euros | www.mrah.be | av. de la Porte de Hal | metro 2, 6: Porte de Hal*

10 SAINT-GILLES

(127 D2–4) (*U E–G 5–7*)
For many decades, immigrants arriving at the Gare du Midi have been shaping the character of *le bas Saint-Gilles*, the lower-lying part of the district around the marketplace, *parvis de Saint-Gilles*. The long-time residents, supporters of the local football club, get together in the *Brasserie de l'Union* (no. 55). A crowd, which would like to think of itself as 'radical chic', congregates in the Art Deco

Brasserie Verschueren (no. 11–13). Amid all the bustle do not under any circumstances miss out on a stroll along *rue Vanderschrick.* Lining the north side is an impressive array of Art Nouveau houses, the finest being *La Porteuse d'Eau* café

The Porte de Hal is the original town wall's only surviving gateway

(on the corner with av. J. Volders). The district's Hôtel de Ville reveals another interesting artistic feature: there is a recently restored ceiling painting in the Salles des Mariages on the first floor by the Symbolist Fernand Khnopff. Behind the fine building starts *le haut Saint-Gilles*, where there are many more Art Nouveau houses. Exhibitions and concerts are regularly staged in the *Maison Pelgrims (rue de Parme 69)* with its enchanting terraced garden. A meeting-place popular among beer and comic devotees is *Moeder Lambic (rue de Savoie 88).* This

is the ideal place to see just how many beers Belgium can offer. *Metro: Parvis de Saint-Gilles*

OTHER QUARTERS

ATOMIUM ★ ● ⚹ (120 C3) (⌘ 0)

In recent years, the symbol for the 1958 World Fair has had a thorough facelift. Thanks to a stainless steel coating, the spheres now gleam brightly even when it's drizzling. The striking structure represents an ice crystal molecule magnified 165 billion times. At night thousands of tiny bulbs illuminate the spheres to create an impressive light show. In the tubes, light cells convey a sense of movement inside a spaceship. Changing exhibitions in the spheres explore the 1950s and contemporary art; the highest one houses a restaurant serving Belgian specialities. A breathtaking panoramic view… and steep prices. *Daily 10am–6pm | admission 11 euros | bd. du Centenaire | www.atomium.be | metro 6: Heysel*

BASILIQUE NATIONALE DU SACRÉ-CŒUR ⚹ (122 A4) (⌘ 0)

On a gently rising hill in the district of Koekelberg stands this neo-Gothic pantheon commissioned by Leopold II in 1905 to honour the nation's heroes. Some 50 or so years later one of the largest churches in the world was completed with some distinctive Art Deco features. Note the similarity with the Basilique du Sacré-Cœur in Paris. Stunning interior, great all-round view from the dome. Tower: *April–Oct daily 9am–5.15pm, Nov–March daily 10am–4.15pm | admission 4 euros | av. du Panthéon/av. des Gloires Nationales | www.basilique.be | metro 2, 6: Simonis*

BOIS DE LA CAMBRE ●
(130 C6) (⌘ J8)

A spur of the 50 sq.km (20 sq.miles) Forêt de Soignes juts out into southern districts of the city like a pointing finger. Le Bois, as the Bruxellois call it, was laid out in English style in 1862 with sandy paths and open spaces. Children love the playground and the roller-skating track, while parents prefer the sunny terrace. The main attraction, though, is the delightful INSIDER TIP *Chalet Robinson* café-restaurant on the island in the lake. Popular specialities here include crêpes and ice-cream, apéritifs and tapas, Brussels brasserie and fusion dishes *(daily noon–11pm | tel. 0 23 72 92 92 | www.chaletrobinson.be | tram 23, 24, 94: Legrand).*

CHÂTEAU DE LAEKEN
(121 F4–5) (⌘ 0)

Built in 1781 as a small-scale summer palace out in the countryside, one hundred years later Leopold II converted it into a proper castle. It is now the king's private residence. For 10 days at the end of April/early May, the Royal Greenhouses are opened up to the public. Exotic plants are cultivated in this vast complex of glass and iron. On the edge of this extensive private estate stand the *Chinese Pavilion* and the *Japanese Tower*.

Lying in the crypt of *Église Notre-Dame-de-Laeken (av. du Parc Royal)* are the tombs of the Belgian kings and almost all family members, while in the *Cimetière de Laeken* behind the church many well-known figures from the 19th century have their last resting place *(daily 9am–5pm | admission free). Av. du Parc Royal /av. Van Praet 44 | Chinese Pavilion and Japanese Tower, Tue–Sun 10am–5pm | admission 4 euros | tram 3: Araucaria*

Chinese Pavilion – imported by Leopold II in the 19th century and crammed full of exotic artefacts

CIMETIÈRE DU DIEWEG ⚜ (0) (🕮 0)

With its numerous Art Nouveau crypts (including that of the architect Paul Hankar), most of which belong to 19th-century banking dynasties, it's as enchanting as an English monastery garden. Although no further burials have been allowed here for some time, the authorities have in exceptional cases granted a special waiver, notably that to Georges Remi, otherwise known as Hergé, the father of the comic strip heroes, Tintin and Snowy. *Daily 8am–4pm | Dieweg 95 | tram 92: Dieweg*

MAISON D'ERASME (0) (🕮 B4)

The celebrated Dutch humanist, Erasmus of Rotterdam, spent a few months of 1521 in this elegant Renaissance mansion. He wrote some 34 philosophical letters at the desk in the library and received visitors in the splendid White Room. None of Erasmus' belongings remain, but the artefacts on view date from the 16th century. Adorning the walls are portraits of Erasmus by Dürer and Holbein and the rooms contain a number of valuable furnishings. There is also a mould of the great man's skull. *Tue–Sun 10am–6pm | admission 1.25 euros | rue du Chapitre 31 | www.erasmushouse.museum | metro 5: Saint-Guidon*

MAISON MAGRITTE (123 D2) (🕮 0)

The painter of hidden desires, scurrilous fantasies and mysterious landscapes, René Magritte, spent the most productive years of his life (1930–54) in a modest apartment in this lower middle-class quarter. Its interior has been faithfully restored and furnished. Photos, memorabilia and some of his works are on view on the first and second floors. *Wed–Sun 10am–6pm | admission 7 euros | rue Esseghem 135 | www.magrittemuseum.be | metro 6: Bockstael*

MUSÉE DAVID ET ALICE VAN BUUREN ● (0) (🕮 0)

The enormously wealthy financier, David van Buuren and his wife Alice, built this Art Deco villa in the district of Uc-

OTHER QUARTERS

cle in 1928. He commissioned only the best Belgian and French workshops to make the furnishings and stained-glass windows. But what is probably of most interest here is the masterpieces brought together by these patrons of the arts.

ing brewery between the months of October and March and visitors during those months get a full tour of the beer production plant. *Mon–Fri 9am–5pm, Sat 10am–5pm | admission 5 euros | rue Gheude 56 | www.cantillon.be | metro 2, 6: Clémenceau*

A journey back to the 1930s – an untouched Art Deco villa that belonged to David and Alice van Buuren

The collection includes works by Pieter Bruegel the Elder, Hercules Seghers, James Ensor and Max Ernst, as well as Belgian Impressionists and Expressionists. Everything has been left hanging exactly as it was when the Buurens were alive. Visitors love the 'Garden of Hearts' and the INSIDER TIP maze modelled on the Cretan labyrinth where the Minotaur dwelt. *Wed–Mon 2pm–5.30pm | admission 10 euros (museum and garden), 5 euros (garden only) | av. Léo Errera 41 | www.museumvanbuuren.com | tram 3, 7: Churchill*

INSIDER TIP MUSÉE DE LA GUEUZE ●
(124 C5) *(ØØ E4)*

At one time breweries dominated the Brussels skyline. One small family developed the idea of documenting the art of *gueuze* production. The museum is also a work-

MUSÉE ROYAL DE L'AFRIQUE CENTRALE ⛄ (133 D3) *(ØØ O)*

This grand building in the elegant suburb of Tervuren was designed in 1904 by the French architect Charles Girault, in neoclassical 'palace' style. Very similar to the Petit Palais built for the Paris 1900 Universal Exhibition, it was commissioned by Leopold II to showcase to the rest of the world the potential of this faraway land. *Due to renovation work the museum is closed until early 2014 | Leuvensesteenweg 13 | Tervuren | www.africamuseum.be | tram: 44 (terminus)*

INSIDER TIP PARC REINE-VERTE
(126 B1) *(ØØ H1)*

In 2007 on a sloping open space between a number of college campuses and the busy rue de Brabant shopping street, the Brussels landscape architect,

Erik Dhont, laid out one of the city's finest parks. Concrete walls contrast with quiet corners and romantic waterfalls, the pathway and steps follow an abstract zigzag pattern through transparent tree plantings. Other features include playgrounds, an organic vegetable garden and the *Cafeteria Pavillon Cannelle (Mon–Fri 11.30am–4pm | www.cannelle.be)* with a lovely terrace. *Daily 9am–sunset | upper entrance: rue des Palais 42 | tram 92, 94: Sainte-Marie | lower entrance: rue Verte 126 | metro: Gare du Nord*

INSIDER TIP **PARC TOURNAY-SOLVAY**
(0) (*M 0*)

Brussels' main park is spread over 7 hectares (17 acres). The original concept for the site dates from 1880, but it was 1930 before it reached its present dimensions. The northern section is given over to uneven grassland, shrubs and rare trees, including a giant copper beech – bridges span narrow gorges. The view from the castle ruins extends over a meadow with gnarled apple trees and a walled vegetable garden. In between, a valley with rampant vegetation surrounds ponds, where duck, geese and swans glide and splash. *Chaussée de la Hulpe 197–203 | tram 94: Boitsfort Gare*

SAINTS-PIERRE-ET-GUIDON
(0) (*M B4–5*)

Few people get to explore in detail the old Gothic church on the former horse-traders' market, but it has a remarkably long history. Inside the chapel's

BOOKS & FILMS

▶ **The Eighth Day** – (1996) Serious social drama filmed in Brussels which tackles society's attitude to those with learning difficulties.

▶ **Tomorrow We Move** – (2004) The Belgian producer Chantal Akerman examines the mother–daughter relationship, when the two find themselves living together again for the first time in many years. Set against the backdrop of the Holocaust in the fashionable quarter around place Georges Brugmann.

▶ **Private Property** – (2006) A drama set in Belgium about a mother in conflict with her estranged husband over the family home. The two sons are caught up in the turmoil. One sub-theme is the relationship between French- and Dutch-speaking Belgians.

▶ **Noah's Child** – (2004; first published in English 2011) is the fourth novel in Eric-Emmanuel Schmitt's series, Cycle de l'Invisible, about childhood and religion. He lives in Brussels.

▶ **Antichrista** – (2003; first published in English 2005) by Amélie Nothomb. Belgian cult writer tells a story about a friendship between two women at Brussels Free University.

▶ **Hergé: The Man Who Created Tintin** by Pierre Assouline. Timed to coincide with Steven Spielberg's long-awaited film 'The Adventures of Tintin: The Secret of the Unicorn' in 2011, here is the first full biography of Hergé available for an English-speaking audience, offering a captivating portrait of a man who revolutionised the art of comics.

crypt, resting on the columns of what is thought to be a Roman villa, is the original tombstone of St Guidon. At noon on St Guidon's Day (12 September), the sun enters through a narrow window high up on the wall, sending a ray of sunlight on to the tomb. *Place de la Vaillance | metro 5: Saint-Guidon*

VILLA EMPAIN (0) (*O*)

In 1930 Michel Polak designed this splendid villa for the industrialist, Louis Empain. The clear architectural lines are typical of Bauhaus style, the sumptuous materials, the decorative wrought ironwork and the lights more Art Deco. Since 2006, the building has been used as a meeting place for artists and scientists from Europe and the Middle East. Attractive cafeteria. *Tue–Sun 10am–6.30pm | admission 10 euros | av. F. D. Roosevelt 67 | www.villaempain.com | tram 94: Solbosch*

WIELS (128 A4) (*D6*)

This stunningly beautiful brewery, stylistically somewhere between Art Deco and Bauhaus, has been converted at great expense into an art gallery. International avant-garde exhibitions are staged in bright and airy rooms. Nice café in the old brewing hall, multi-cultural atmosphere. *Wed–Sun 11am–6pm, Sun 11am–5pm | admission 6 euros | av. van Volxem 354 | www.wiels.org | tram 82: Wielemans*

OUTSIDE THE CITY

FONDATION FOLON (133 D3) (*O*)

Jean-Michel Folon (1934–2005) enjoyed a worldwide reputation as an illustrator. His abstract figures in watercolours often included conventionally dressed 'everyman' figure alone in an empty landscape or else in an urban setting surrounded by skyscrapers. His drawings were regularly seen on posters and on the covers of international magazines. He donated over 500 works and his archive to a foundation, now accommodated in the estate of the grand Domaine Solvay in the suburb of La Hulpe. A well-stocked shop, nice café-restaurant with a lovely terrace. *Tue–Sun 10am–6pm | admission 7.50 euros | Ferme du Château de La Hulpe, Drève*

RELAX & ENJOY

The avant-garde architects of Brussels didn't just build mansions for wealthy patrons, they also built swimming pools. The ● *Piscine Victor Boin* dates from 1905. Plenty of light enters through the glass roof and, if the weather is fine, it can be opened up. Some 260 changing cabins spread over two galleries and the elegant staircase are reflected in this white-tiled pool, which is of Olympic dimensions. Relaxation guaranteed – choose from the Turkish or Russian steambath, jacuzzi or massage. *Swimming pool: Mon–Tue, Thu–Fri 8am–7pm, Wed 2pm–7pm, Sat 9am–6pm (school holidays: Mon–Fri noon–7pm, Sat noon–6pm) | admission 2 euros | steambaths: men Mon, Thu 8am–8.30pm, Sat 9am–7.30, women Tue 8am–7.30, Fri 8am–8.30pm | admission 18 euros | (128 C3) (F6) rue de la Perche 38 | tel. 02 53 90 61 5 | metro: Horta de la Ramée 6A, 1310 La Hulpe | www.fondationfolon.be | car or TEC-Bus 366 from av. du Général de Gaulle (Étangs d'Ixelles)*

JARDIN BOTANIQUE NATIONAL DE BELGIQUE (132 C2) (*∅ 0*)

The National Botanic Garden of Belgium, which covers some 9,200 hectares (22,500 acres), is situated in Meise 12km (7.5 miles) north of Brussels. Around 18,000 plant species are cultivated there and in the *Palais des Plantes*, a miniature town of 30 glass greenhouses (13 of which are open to the public). One of the special themes is the flora of central Africa, in particular the cultivation of particular coffee varieties. Attractive shop, where seeds, plants and honey are sold. *April–Sept daily 9.30am–5.30pm, Oct–March daily 9.30am–4.30pm | admission 4 euros | Domaine de Bouchout, Nieuwelaan 38, 1860 Meise | www.jardin botanique.be | by car, De-Lijn-Bus 250, 251 from Bruxelles-Nord station*

MUSÉE HERGÉ (133 E4) (*∅ 0*)

Situated in the new university town of Louvain-la-Neuve (25km/15 miles south of Brussels), this stunning museum, dating from 2009 and designed by top French architect Christian de Portzamparc, emerges from woodland like the bow of a ship. Fans of the Belgian comic writer and illustrator (1907–1983), from whose pen came Tintin, Snowy and Captain Haddock, will find here, not just many original drawings and first prints, but also personal belongings of Georges Remi, otherwise known as Hergé. Well-stocked shop. *Tue–Fri 10.30am–5.30pm, Sat/Sun 10am–6pm | admission 9.50 euros | rue du Labrador 26, 1348 Louvain-la-Neuve | www.museeherge.com | car or train (from all Brussels stations) to Louvain-la-Neuve-Université*

Bronze sculpture of a farmer sowing seeds – in the Botanical Garden

WATERLOO (132 C3) (*∅ 0*)

On 18 June 1815 Napoleon was finally defeated at the Battle of Waterloo, some 20km (12 miles) south of Brussels. The main sight here is the *Butte du Lion*, a 43m-high (141ft) man-made conical mound topped by a lion monument. From the top of the hill, it is easy to gain an impression of what happened on the battlefield, while at the foot a huge fresco, known as the Waterloo Cyclorama, shows how, in the days before the moving image, such dramatic events were portrayed to the public. A new visitor centre should be completed for the 200th anniversary of this seminal moment in European history in 2015 – and of course a full re-enactment is planned. *April–Oct 9.30am–6.30pm, Nov–March 10am–5pm | admission 8.70 euros | Centre du visiteur, route du Lion 315 | www.water loo1815.be | car or TEC bus W and 365 from Bruxelles-Midi station*

FOOD & DRINK

In Brussels they prefer breakfast-lite. A *café au lait*, a slice of bread and jam, perhaps a croissant. Lunch is more substantial, but in the evening it's more like a feast.

The concept of the *déjeuner* in the form of a working lunch still exists, but only rarely is it a lavish four-course meal with aperitifs and copious amounts of wine. Shorter, lighter lunches with just two courses – either starter and main course, or main course and dessert, a couple of glasses of wine and water followed by coffee are now the norm. In the evening the locals prefer to eat out in stylish surroundings but casually dressed. The current trend is for a southern Mediterranean variant of jeune cuisine, a re-interpretation of traditional recipes, and also

for Japanese cooking. One vital ingredient is top-quality olive oil; vegetarian dishes are also becoming increasingly popular. *Déjeuner* or lunch begins at 1pm, but in the evening restaurants only start filling up after 8pm, sometimes even later. *Dîner* – the evening meal – usually consists of three courses: starter, main course and dessert. These are often packaged together as a set meal at an 'all-in' price. Making a table reservation is recommended.

CAFÉS & TEAROOMS

INSIDER TIP ▶ LE BALMORAL
(129 E5) (*ψ G8*)
Café furnished in 1950s style with rock and roll music from that era. Milk shakes

Photo: Fish restaurants along Quai aux Briques

Moules-frites or caviar and truffles – Brussels can offer tasty treats to suit every palate and every purse

a speciality. This favourite haunt of the smart set also has highly coveted tables for al fresco dining. *Closed Mon | place Georges Brugmann 21 | bus 60: Georges Brugmann*

CAFÉ BEBO (125 D5) *(⌂ F4)*
Good breakfasts served in this fashionable café-bar. Later inexpensive daily specials and delicious tapas meals with a thoughtfully selected range of beers and wines. *Closed Sun | av. de Stalingrad 2 | metro: Anneessens*

CAFÉ DU VAUDEVILLE (125 E3) *(⌂ G3)*
Elegant café and restaurant in the Galeries Saint-Hubert. Terrace, lounges with plush leather seats on the first floor. Window seats very popular. *Daily | galerie de la Reine 11 | metro 1, 5: Gare Centrale*

INSIDER TIP COMPTOIR FLORIAN (126 B6) *(⌂ H5)*
On the menu in this tiny Art Nouveau café-bar are the finest teas and pâtisserie. Give the *thé de Bruxelles* with its speculaas biscuit aroma a try. *Closed Sun*

and Mon | rue St.-Boniface 17 | ,metro 2, 6: Porte de Namur

CORICA ★ (125 E3) (*m* G3)

Freshly roasted here are some 24 varieties of fine coffees, imported exclusively from family-run businesses. In addition you can sample and buy 64 unusual types

aux Briques 24 | www.frederic-blondeel. com | metro 1, 5: Sainte-Catherine

GAUDRON (129 E5) (*m* G8)

Smart bar in a fashionable quarter; also serves snacks. The terrace is a hot-spot, especially at weekends. Daily | place Georges Brugmann 3 | tram 92: Darwin

Tartes, pastries and cakes to die for – Wittamer, Brussels' finest pâtissier

of tea from the company that supplies Michelin-starred restaurants. Closed Sun | marché aux Poulets 49 | metro: Bourse

LE FRAMBOISIER DORÉ (130 A3) (*m* H6)

Nice ice-cream parlour. Flavours include basil, lavender, thyme and speculaas biscuit. Also kriek beer sorbets. Wed–Fri 11.30am–7pm, Sat and Sun 12.30pm–7pm | rue du Bailli 35 | tram 94: Bailli

FRÉDÉRIC BLONDEEL (125 D2) (*m* F2)

Finest varieties of tea and coffee to accompany unusual pralines. In summer home-made ice cream. Closed Mon | quai

INSIDER TIP LEBEAU SOLEIL (125 E5) (*m* G4)

Delicious breakfast, lunch, afternoon tea and aperitifs in the studio of a loquacious Greek instrument maker. Favourite weekend haunt of late-risers. Closed Mon | rue de Rollebeek 25–27 | www.lebeau-soleil. com | metro 1, 5: Gare Centrale

MAMY LOUISE (129 E–F1) (*m* G5)

Smart meeting place in an elegant Upper Town shopping quarter. Delicious pastries, chunky sandwiches and light snacks. The terrace is for seeing and being seen. Closed Sun | rue Jean Stas 12 | metro 2, 6: Louise

WITTAMER (125 E5) *(ᗰ G4)*

The café run by Brussels' master pâtissier has views over place du Grand Sablon and an elegant lounge on the first floor. Matching clientele. *Closed Mon | place du Grand Sablon 12–13 | tram 92, 94: Petit Sablon*

RESTAURANTS: EXPENSIVE

BOUCHÉRY (128 C6) *(ᗰ E8)*

The young Breton chef Damien Bouchery specialises in unusual combinations of fish and meat, herbs and spices. Elegant setting, smart clientele. *Closed for lunch Sat, closed Sun and Mon | chaussée d'Alsemberg 842 | tel. 0 23 32 37 74 | www.bouchery-restaurant.be | tram 51: Rittweger*

CHOU (126 B6) *(ᗰ H4)*

Brilliantly designed restaurant, one notable feature being the glass floor between the dining room and wine cellar. Ingenious cuisine and excellent wines from Burgundy and the Rhône valley. *Closed Sun and Mon | place de Londres 4 | tel. 0 25 11 92 38 | www.restaurantchou.eu | metro 2, 6: Trône*

COSPAIA (129 F1) *(ᗰ G5)*

Beautifully furnished in black and white, bar and lounge with jet set glamour, nice terrace; light modern cuisine with exotic notes. Good selection of wines and champagnes. *Closed Sun | tel. 0 25 13 03 03 | www.cospaia.be | rue Capitaine Crespel 1 | metro 2, 6: Louise*

NOTOS ★ (130 A3) *(ᗰ H6)*

Amazing Greek nouvelle cuisine, accompanied by the best Hellenic barrique wines. Art Deco surroundings, separate tables for those seeking privacy. This place has caused such a stir among Brussels foodies that you are advised to make your reservation days in advance. *Closed Sun, closed for lunch Mon | rue de Livourne 154 | tel. 0 25 13 29 59 | www.notos.be | tram 94: Bailli*

★ **Corica**
Coffees and teas for Michelin-starred chefs and connoisseurs → p. 58

★ **Notos**
Top notch Greek cuisine in an Art Nouveau setting → p. 59

★ **Kwint**
Offers the finest in caviar, truffles and art, plus a panoramic view over the city → p. 62

★ **Callens Café**
Brussels cuisine – fresh and fashionable → p. 63

★ **Nonbe Daigaku**
Japanese specialities straight out of grandma's recipe book → p. 62

★ **Bon-Bon**
Creative cuisine from a culinary superstar → p. 60

★ **Comme chez Soi**
Heaven for fine diners, plus an excellent wine list → p. 60

★ **Sea Grill**
One of the world's finest sea food restaurants → p. 60

MARCO POLO HIGHLIGHTS

ROUGE TOMATE (130 B3) (🛱 H6)

Creative *cuisine minceur* (low calorie meals for slimmers) with organic produce in a beautifully restyled patrician house. Large paintings in warm colours adorn the walls. Mainly vegetarian dishes with copious amounts of olive oil; pretty garden. A favourite haunt of Brussels' *bobos*. Reservation essential. *Closed for lunch Sat, closed Sun | av. Louise 190 | tel. 0 26 47 70 44 | www.rougetomate.com | tram 94: Bailli*

LE STIRWEN (127 D6) (🛱 K5)

Fine regional specialities from Brussels and southwest France served in this glorious Art Nouveau restaurant on the edge of the European quarter. Favoured by devotees of brain, heart, sheep's head and tripe. *Closed Sat and Sun | chaussée Saint-Pierre 15–17 | tel. 0 26 40 85 41 | www.stirwen.be | metro 1, 5: Maelbeek*

LE VIGNOBLE DE MARGOT 🥬 (0) (🛱 0)

Fresh seafood and fish dishes with a Mediterranean touch, served in a Bauhaus showpiece with a view of the lake in the gardens. An idyllic spot at sunset, especially on the terrace. *Closed for lunch Sat, closed Sun | av. de Tervueren 368 | tel. 0 27 79 23 23 | www.levigno*

GOURMET RESTAURANTS

Bon-Bon ★ (0) (🛱 0)

Every day culinary superstar Christophe Hardiquest creates innovative, contrasting dishes, including oxtail and pork cheek. Menus from 67 euros. *Closed for lunch Sat, closed Sun and Mon | av. de Tervueren 453 | tel. 0 23 46 66 15 | www.bon-bon.be | tram 44: Trois*

Chalet de la Forêt (132 C3) (🛱 0)

Pascal de Valkeneer serves exciting seasonal dishes in the stylish setting of this former country auberge. Wonderful terrace in the garden, discreet salons. Menus from 72 euros. *Closed Sat and Sun | Drève de Lorraine 43 | tel. 0 23 74 54 16 | www.lechaletdelaforet.be | taxi or car*

Comme chez Soi ★ (125 D5) (🛱 F4)

Pierre Wynants, the doyen of Belgian haute cuisine, has passed on the management of this 'institution' to his son-in-law Lionel Rigolet who is cautiously leading the restaurant in a new direction. Still has the finest wine cellar in the whole of Brussels, superb service. Menus from 87 euros. *Closed for lunch Wed, closed Sun and Mon | place Rouppe 23 | tel. 0 25 12 29 21 | www.commechezsoi.be | metro: Anneessens*

Sea Grill ★ (125 F3) (🛱 G2)

Imaginative, light preparation of fish and seafood by head chef Yves Mattagne, regarded by many not only as the best in Belgium, but the best in the world. Classy service. Menus from 60 euros. *Closed all day Sat and Sun | rue du Fossé-aux-Loups 47 | Radisson-SAS-Hotel | tel. 0 22 12 08 00 | www.seagrill.be | metro: De Brouckère*

Villa Lorraine (0) (🛱 0)

An old ivy-covered villa on the edge of the Forêt de Soignes. Creative nouvelle cuisine, discreet atmosphere. Popular with Brussels financiers and politicians. Menu from 85 euros. *Closed all day Sun | av. du Vivier d'Oie 75 | tel. 0 23 74 31 63 | www.villalorraine.be | bus 41: Gendarmes*

Comme chez Soi – haute cuisine heading in a new direction; boasts the city's finest wine cellar

bledemargot.be | tram 44: Dépôt de Woluwé

RESTAURANTS: MODERATE

AL BARMAKI (125 E4) *(𝄞 G3)*

It may be Brussels' oldest Lebanese restaurant, but it is still among the best. Try out a wide range of delicious *meze* dishes in elegant surroundings. *Opens 7pm Mon–Sat | rue des Eperonniers 67 | tel. 0 25 13 08 34 | www.albarmaki.be | metro 1, 5: Gare Centrale*

BUCA DI BACCO (0) *(𝄞 0)*

Light Italian cuisine served in a wonderful Art Nouveau setting. Always full. *Closed for lunch Sat, closed Mon | tel. 0 22 42 42 30 | www.bucadibacco.be | av. Louis Bertrand 65 | tram 92: Saint-Servais*

CAFÉ DES SPORES (129 D4) *(𝄞 F7)*

Countless fine wines to sample in this old wine store, but there is another attraction: the many delicious INSIDER TIP mushroom dishes. *Closed Sun | chaussée d'Alsemberg 103 | tel. 0 25 34 13 03 | www. cafedesspores.be | metro: Horta*

CHEZ MAX (130 A5) *(𝄞 H7)*

Excellent brasserie in a former post office serving seasonal French dishes and a good selection of wines. *Closed for lunch Sat–Tue, closed Sun and Mon | chaussée de Waterloo 550 A | tel. 0 23 44 42 32 | www.chezmaxrestaurant.be | bus 60: Tenbosch*

INSIDER TIP LE DIPTYQUE (0) *(𝄞 0)*

Stylishly-designed, upmarket brasserie in the entrance hall of the Villa Lorraine. Can cater for diners with big appetites or those in need of a quick snack. Optional side dishes and sauces. All produce sourced from top suppliers. Bar and smokers' lounge open until 1am. Very popular, so reservation essential. *Closed Sun and Mon | av. du Vivier d'Oie i 75 | tel. 0 23 74 31 63 | www.villalorraine.be | bus 41: Gendarmes*

KWINT ★ ♨ (125 F4) (📖 G3)

Beneath the vaulted ceiling hangs a spectacular copper sculpture by conceptual artist Arne Quinze. The view over the city is equally impressive. Gastronomically, everything revolves around caviar and truffles. Beautiful terrace, fashionable lounge bar – reservations essential. *Closed Sun | Mont des Arts 1 | tel. 0 25 05 95 95 | www.kwintbrussels. be | metro 1, 5: Gare Centrale*

NONBE DAIGAKU ★ (131 D5) (📖 K8)

Modest layout but the very best in Japanese cuisine. Sashimi, sushi and soups served at lunchtime. In the evening, dishes from grandma's recipe book. Reservation essential. *Closed Sun and Mon | av. Buyl 31 | tel. 0 26 49 21 49 | tram 7, 25, 94: Buyl*

PARK SIDE BRASSERIE (127 E5) (📖 K4)

Glamorous furnishings in keeping with the Brussels specialities on the menu. Lovely view, cosmopolitan clientele. *Daily | av. de la Joyeuse Entrée 24 | tel. 0 22 38 08 08 | www.restoparkside.be | metro 1, 5: Schuman*

IN 'T SPINNEKOPKE (125 D3) (📖 F3)

In an elderly building full of charming paraphernalia, serving typical Brussels-style dishes of meat braised in beer (e. g. *lapin à la gueuze* or rabbit in *gueuze*); the chef has also been trying out new ideas such as *perdreau à la bière de framboise* or partridge in raspberry beer. In addition, over 100 strong beers and abbey beers to choose from. Clientele a mixture of long-standing Brussels residents and young *bobos*. Terrace. *Closed for lunch Sat | place du Jardin-aux-fleurs 1 | tel. 0 25 11 86 95 | www.spinnekopke.be | metro: Anneessens*

Partridge in raspberry beer – In't Spinnekopke restaurant specialises in beer-braised dishes

TAVERNE DU PASSAGE (125 E3) (📖 G3)

Traditional brasserie in pure Art Deco style; diners served by waiters dressed fittingly in white jackets with gold braid. Typical Brussels specialities (e.g. calves' sweetbreads), excellent wine list. Terrace in the heart of the splendid Galeries Saint-Hubert. *Closed June and July and all day Wed and Thu | Galerie de la Reine 30 | tel. 0 25 12 37 31 | www.tavernedu passage.com | metro: De Brouckère*

TOUCAN BRASSERIE (130 A5) *(🌃 G7)*
Stylish and popular, this venue offers creative Franco-Belgian cuisine. Good service, great atmosphere, reservation essential. Attractive terrace for coffee and aperitifs. *Daily | av. Louis Lepoutre 1 | tel. 0 23 45 30 17 | www.toucanbrasserie. com | bus 60: Tenbosch*

THE WOOD 😊 **(130 C6)** *(🌃 J8)*
This former forester's lodge occupies an idyllic spot in the Bois de la Cambre forest. Mediterranean or Asian-inspired light cuisine with seasonal, regionally-sourced organic produce. Nice terrace. From 11pm onwards fashionable bar and disco. *Closed for lunch Sat, closed Mon | av. de Flore 3–4 | tel. 0 26 40 19 68 | www.thewood.be | tram 94: Solbosch*

RESTAURANTS: BUDGET

ARCADI (125 E3) *(🌃 G3)*
This cosy restaurant is ideal for a meal before or after the opera or the cinema. Slightly cramped and always full. Favourites include the *tartes* prepared to Middle Eastern, Italian or Provencale recipes, lots of vegetarian dishes too. *Daily | rue d'Arenberg 1b | tel. 0 25 11 33 43 | metro 1, 5: Gare Centrale*

CAFÉ PANISSE (129 F4) *(🌃 G7)*
Even when it's raining, there is always a cheerful, Provencale atmosphere here. Pastis, pizza and pasta, plus service that's sure to revive holiday memories. *Closed for lunch Sat and Sun | rue du Tabellion 31 | tel. 0 25 39 39 10 | www.cafepanisse. com | tram 81: Trinité*

CALLENS CAFÉ ⭐ **(130 B5)** *(🌃 J8)*
Stylishly-designed rooms, tables on the lawn in summer. Typical Brussels brasserie fare, but always with fresh salad

or vegetables. Popular meeting place, good service. If you haven't booked a table (in time), you can wait in the nice bar closed for lunch *Sat, closed Sun | av. Louise 480 (entrance at the rear of the building, av. E. De Mot) | tel. 0 26 47 66 68 | www.callenscafe.be | tram 94: Legrand*

LOW BUDGET

▶ The cool and stylish *Café National (Mon–Fri noon–2pm | (125 E2) (🌃 G2) boulevard Jacqmain 111–115 | in the Théâtre National)* serves an oriental buffet at lunchtimes for 10 euros. Before performances from 5.30pm a meal costs 12 euros.

▶ One popular fish stall is *De Noordzee (Mon–Thu 10am–6pm, Fri–Sun 10am–9pm | (125 D3) (🌃 F2) rue Sainte Catherine 45)*, for fresh and inexpensive delicacies.

▶ The 🍽 cafeteria in the Royal Library *(Mon–Fri 9am–3.15 pm | (125 F4) (🌃 G3) Bibliothèque Royale (Level +5), Mont des Arts)* is open to all. Affordable daily specials and sandwiches, and the fine view comes free of charge.

▶ Cheap and cheerful options in Brussels are the soup bars, which also serve sandwiches. A bowl of soup costs between 3 and 6 euros, e.g. the *Bio Lounge (Mon–Fri noon–4pm | (126 B3) (🌃 H2–3) rue de l'Enseignement 116–120)* and *Oups (Mon–Fri 9am–5pm | (130 B3) (🌃 J6) rue Lesbroussart 13)*.

LOCAL SPECIALITIES

▶ **anguilles au vert** – eel in parsley sauce
▶ **asperges à la flamande** – asparagus with a butter, egg and parsley sauce
▶ **boudins à la bruxelloise** – white pudding and black pudding in an apple compôte
▶ **cabillaud à la bière** – cod with onions and dried meat, cooked in beer
▶ **caricolles** – sea snails in a spicy stock
▶ **chicons (or witloof)** – chicory in a creamy sauce or au gratin
▶ **coucou de Bruxelles à la bière** – free-range chicken with dried meat and onions, braised in beer
▶ **crème bruxelloise** – cream of brussels sprout soup (photo right)
▶ **croquettes de crevettes** – deep-fried prawn croquettes in a béchamel sauce
▶ **faisan à la brabanconne** – braised pheasant with chicory
▶ **gueuze** – slightly sour beer, matured in the same way as champagne
▶ **half-en-half** – aperitif made with sparkling wine and white wine
▶ **kriek** – gueuze with cherry juice
▶ **lapin à la gueuze** – rabbit braised in sour Brussels beer
▶ **lièvre à la royale** – roast hare in a blood and Burgundy sauce
▶ **merlans à la bruxelloise** – fillet of whiting in a cream and abbey cheese sauce
▶ **moules-frites** –mussels and chips (photo left)
▶ **poutargue** – toast with creamed fish roe and butter
▶ **ris de veau Archiduc** – deep-fried veal sweetbreads with boiled vegetables
▶ **stoemp** – mashed potato with vegetables
▶ **tartine au fromage blanc** – farmhouse bread with a curd cheese spread, onions and radishes

LE FOURNEAU (125 D2) *(ᗰ F2)*
Diners sit around the open kitchen and can order nibbles with prices calculated by weight. Always busy; no reservations. *Closed Sun and Mon | place Sainte-Catherine 8 | tel. 0 25 13 10 02 | metro 1, 5: Sainte-Catherine*

INSIDER TIP L'HORLOGE DU SUD **(126 C6)** *(ᗰ J5)*
In this brasserie a super-friendly young team prepares African, Caribbean and Brazilian specialities. Regular concerts and screenings in the room above the restaurant. *Closed for lunch Sat, closed*

Sun | rue du Trône 141 | tel. 0 25 12 18 64 | www.horlogedusud.be | metro 2, 6: Trône

KIF-KIF CAFÉ (130 C4) (*Ŵ J6*)

The Arab owner has teamed up with an Israeli chef. She prepares imaginative *meze,* hearty couscous and aromatic *tajines*. Fine range of pastries. Stylish interior and INSIDERTIP secluded terrace – a very popular spot. *Daily | square de Biarritz 1 | tel. 0 26 44 18 10 | tram 81: Flagey*

LE PERROQUET (125 E5) (*Ŵ G4*)

Not a lot of room to move in this splendid Art Nouveau setting. Wide selection of delicious salads, good house wines. Young, lively clientele. Terrace. *Daily | rue Watteau 31 | tel. 0 25 12 99 22 | tram 92, 94: Petit Sablon*

LE PETIT CANON (130 B3) (*Ŵ H6*)

Fashionable wine bar, also serves beer, cocktails and spirits. Tasty nibbles and hearty daily specials. Likeable bobo clientele. *Closed Sun | rue Lesbroussart 91 | tel. 0 26 40 38 34 | www.lepetitcanon.be | tram 81: Dautzenberg*

PLATTESTEEN (125 E4) (*Ŵ F3*)

No-nonsense brasserie with terrace; simple dishes such as soups, mashed potatoes with vegetables, steak. Inexpensive daily specials. *Daily | tel. 0 25 12 82 03 | rue Marché-au-Charbon | metro: Bourse*

QUENTIN PAIN ET VIN (129 F4) (*Ŵ G7*)

Cool wine bar in the fashionable place du Châtelain quarter, inventive sandwiches, delicious nibbles. INSIDERTIP Champagne bar and disco on Thursday. *Closed Sun and Mon | rue du Page 7 | tel. 0 25 37 85 97 | tram 94: Bailli*

RACONTE-MOI DES SALADES (130 A4) (*Ŵ H6*)

Situated in an old building in Brussels' most fashionable square, pretty setting with garden. Wide selection of salads and good pasta dishes. *Closed Sun | place du Châtelain 19 | tel. 0 25 34 27 27 | tram 94: Bailli*

TROP BON 🕑 (130 C3) (*Ŵ J6*)

Delicious, healthy dishes, salads and fruit juices from organically-sourced produce. Relaxed atmosphere, always full. *Open for lunch only, Mon–Fri | chaussée de Vleurgat 1 | tel. 0 26 40 40 57 | tram 81: Flagey*

Fresh seafood in Brussels

SHOPPING

CITY WHERE TO START?
For fashionistas the first port of call is **rue Antoine Dansaert** and its many smart boutiques, but also **avenue Louise**. You will find the best antiques and finest pralines around **place du Grand Sablon**. Bargain hunters will have a field day in the **Marolles quarter**. Galleries and markets are to be found throughout the city.

Many people remain loyal to the old-fashioned, family-run shop, others head straight for the "all under one roof" department store. Whatever your preference, Brussels can offer both in plenty, plus a wide range of other slightly more unorthodox shopping experiences.

The most popular shopping street in all of Belgium by a long way is the pedestrianised *rue Neuve* (125 E2–3) *(ᗰ G2)* and the huge shopping mall, City 2, the largest urban retail complex in Belgium. In *rue de Brabant* (126 A1) *(ᗰ H1)* near Gare du Nord, Arab, Jewish, Pakistani and Turkish traders have transformed the area into a veritable INSIDER TIP▶ bazaar, which at the weekend attracts a cosmopolitan crowd of shopaholics from what seems like half of Europe. Most of the shops in the historic *Galeries Saint-Hubert* (125 E3) *(ᗰ G3)* are distinctly upmarket. Fashionistas from all over the world flock to ★ *rue Antoine Dansaert* and its side streets (125 D2–3) *(ᗰ F2–3)*. It is here that famous Belgian couturiers such as Jean-Paul Knott or Martin Margiela and up-and-coming talents run smart

The city loves to boast about its beers and exquisite chocolates, but the shopping streets of Brussels have much, much more to offer

boutiques. Other swanky spots are *place du Grand Sablon* (125 E5) *(𝄢 G4)* with an array of fine confectionery and antique shops, and *rue de Namur* (126 A5) *(𝄢 G–H4)* between the Upper and Lower Town. The Upper Town is the home of international designer brands ranging from Armani to Zegna on *boulevard de Waterloo* (126 A6) *(𝄢 G–H5)*. The area around *rue du Bailli* and *place du Châtelain* (130 A3–4) *(𝄢 G–H6)* plus *place Georges Brugmann* (129 E5) *(𝄢 G8)* and environs tend to cater for well-heeled 20-somethings. Also exclusive but less expensive is *avenue Lou-ise* (130 A1–2) *(𝄢 G–H 5–6)* with the flagship stores for fashionable Belgian brands, such as Bellerose, Chine, Mer du Nord or Xandres. Most shops are open Monday to Saturday from 10am to 6.30pm, but bakeries, butchers' shops and corner shops stay open on Sunday.

BOOKSHOPS – NEW & SECOND-HAND

FILIGRANES (126 B4) *(𝄢 H3)*
The city's largest bookshop with a special department for discounted books. **INSIDER TIP** Children's zone, cafeteria

and wine bar. Also open on Sunday. *Av. des Arts 39–40 | metro: Arts-Loi*

PEINTURE FRAÎCHE (130 A4) *(G6)*

The shop offers an excellent selection of art books, including cut-price editions and there's a pleasant atmosphere here too. Only open Thu–Sat. *Rue du Tabellion 10 | tram 81: Trinité*

PÊLE-MÊLE (125 D4) *(F3)p*

Enormous shop with old books and comics of all genres, plus LPs and CDs at bar-

TROPISMES
(125 E3) *(G3)*

The best place for French and Belgian literature and the humanities. There's always the chance of meeting top writers. *Galerie des Princes 11 | Galeries Saint-Hubert | metro: De Brouckère*

COMICS

LA BANDE DES SIX NEZ ★
(130 C1) *(H5)*

One of the oldest shops devoted to the

Atelier de Moulages – piled high with plaster of Paris, pure white or painted

gain prices. *Bd. Maurice Lemonnier 55 | metro: Anneessens*

QUARTIERS LATINS (125 F2) *(G2)*

This nice bookshop specialises in small Belgian publishers and on the city of Brussels. Inexpensive books on photography. *Place des Martyrs 14 | Galeries Saint-Hubert | metro: Rogier*

'ninth art'. The latest comics and comic books, antiquarian first editions and original drawings. Good selection of lithographs and ephemera. *Chaussée de Wavre 179 | bus 34: Parnasse*

BRÜSEL (125 E3) *(F3)*

A very wide range of works published by small, independent houses, often by refreshing, new authors. Friendly staff. *Bd. Anspach 100 | metro: Bourse*

BEER & WINE

BEER MANIA ★ (126 B6) (ᗕ *H5*)
More than 400 types of beer including light and dark beers from Belgian abbeys, such as Chimay and Orval. All beers brewed organically using traditional methods. Knowledgeable staff. Tastings available. *Chaussée de Wavre 174 | metro 2, 6: Porte de Namur*

MIG'S WORLD WINES (129 F2) (ᗕ *G5*)
Fine wines from 20 countries, including Mexico and Uruguay, the highlights being Belgian *grands crus*, prestige wines from famous vineyards. Friendly, knowledgeable staff, bottles attractively gift-wrapped. *Chaussée de Charleroi 43 | tram 92: Stéphanie*

GIFTS & SOUVENIRS

ATELIER DE MOULAGES ★ (127 F5) (ᗕ *L4*)
The workshop is situated at the rear of the Royal Museums of Art and History. Reasonably priced casts of fine originals, ranging from little scarabs to life-size Apollos, pure white or faithful reproductions of the original. *Tue–Fri 9.30am–noon, 1.30pm–4pm | Parc du Cinquantenaire 10 | metro 1, 5: Mérode*

INSIDER TIP LE BRIDGEUR (130 A3) (ᗕ *H6*)
The 'bridge player' offers a huge selection of card and board games. *Rue du Bailli 61 | tram 94: Bailli*

MANUFACTURE BELGE DE DENTELLES (125 E2) (ᗕ *G3*)
Founded in 1810, this business is still making hand-made Belgian bobbin lace. Expensive. *Galerie de la Reine 6–8 | metro: De Brouckère*

PLAIZIER (125 E4) (ᗕ *G3*)
Postcards with photos of old Brussels, booklets and posters on Art Nouveau, weird and wonderful stationery and toys. Ideal for small gifts. *Rue des Eperonniers 50 | metro 1, 5: Gare Centrale*

MARCO POLO HIGHLIGHTS

★ **La Bande des Six Nez**
An unusual comic shop, also selling originals → p. 68

★ **Beer Mania**
Belgium's best beers with the chance to sample prior to purchase → p. 69

★ **Atelier de Moulages**
Inexpensive casts of classical masterpieces.→ p. 69

★ **Place du Jeu de Balle**
Huge, colourful flea market → p. 70

★ **Ut pictura musica**
Posh music shop selling music by small, European classical recording labels → p. 71

★ **Rue Antoine Dansaert**
Boutique quarter populated by fashionable designers → p. 66

★ **Dandoy**
For heavenly confectionery → p. 73

★ **Marcolini**
Unusual pralines and finest dark chocolate → p. 73

INTERIOR DESIGN & HOME FURNISHINGS

INSIDER TIP ▶ SEPTANTESEPT
(129 F4) (*∅ G7*)
Unusual decorations and home furnishings, imaginative children's toys, innovative gadgets – only by young Belgian designers and artists. *Rue du Page 77 | www.septantesept.be | tram 81: Trinité*

INTERIOR DESIGN & HOME FURNISHINGS

DÉPÔT-DESIGN (124 C2) (*∅ B2*)
Heavily discounted designer furniture, including copies of Costes chairs by Philippe Starck and side tables by Eileen Grey, are on sale in this former warehouse. *Quai du Hainaut 19 | metro 1, 5: Comte de Flandre*

HOME OF COOKING (125 E3) (*∅ G2*)
Amateur and professional chefs will be in their element here. Quality Belgian products and countless recipe books to encourage you back into the kitchen. *Rue Léopold 3 | metro: De Brouckère*

INSIDER TIP ▶ THE LINEN HOUSE
(125 F5) (*∅ G4*)
This tiny shop is upholding the tradition of Belgian linen. An impressive selection of original bed and table linen; material sold by the metre. *Rue Bodenbroeck 10 | tram 92, 94: Petit Sablon*

ART GALLERIES

INSIDER TIP ▶ AUTOMATESGALERIE
(129 F2) (*∅ G5*)
This small gallery specialises in the world's tiniest works of art, some with moving parts. A delight for children of all ages. *Chaussée de Charleroi 24–26 | www.automatesgalerie.be | tram 92, 94: Stéphanie*

CONTRETYPE (129 E5) (*∅ G7*)
Leading photo gallery. Exhibitions of works by young Belgian and international artists staged here on a regular basis. Good selection of specialist literature. *Av. de la Jonction 1 | www.contretype.org | tram 92: Ma Campagne*

DÉRAPAGES (130 A3) (*∅ G6*)
Square paintings by over thirty artists, each one available in four formats. Prices between 49–247 euros subject to format, framed 71–289 euros. *Rue du Bailli 98 | www.derapages.com | tram 81: Trinité*

MARKETS

ANTIQUES
★ *Place du Jeu de Balle* in the Marolles quarter (125 D6) (*∅ F4*) daily 6am–2pm. The range is best on weekday mornings, the clientele best on Saturday and Sunday around lunch-time.
Place du Grand Sablon (125 E5) (∅ G4*)*, Sat 9am–6pm, Sun 9am–2pm. Better quality articles.

FOOD
Gare du Midi (124 B–C5) (∅ E5*)* Sun 6am–1pm. This is a must. Flemish vegetable growers and traders from all over the world. Immigrants, bohemians and tourists mingle here. A fantastic atmosphere, but produce quality mediocre.
Place du Châtelain (129 F4) (∅ H6*)* Wed 2pm–7pm. Many organic farmers from Brabant (excellent dairy products, homemade jams, delicious tartes), and it is worth watching the yuppie crowd who know their way around inside out.
Place Flagey (130 C3) (∅ J6*)* Tue–Sun 7am–1pm, Sat and Sun artists and university crowd. *Place Sainte-Catherine (125 D3) (*∅ F2*)* daily 7am–5pm.

INSIDER TIP *Place Wiener* (O) (*m O*) Sun 9am–2pm, in the Watermael-Boitsfort district, home of artists and the intelligentsia. Homegrown organic products, wide selection of cheeses made from unpasteurised milk. Delicacies from Italy and North Africa, great herbs and spices.

FASHION

AMBIORIX (126 A5) (*m H4*)
Belgium's last shoe factory designs classic and fashion shoes for men and women. Hand-crafted from top-quality leather, all at very reasonable prices. *Rue de Namur 74 | www.ambiorix.be | metro 2, 6: Porte de Namur*

LES ENFANTS D'EDOUARD (130 B3) (*m H6*)
Huge selection of top quality designer clothes that have been worn (but only briefly). Extremely good value. *Av. Louise 175–179 | tram 94: Bailli*

NATAN (126 A5) (*m H4*)
Couturier Edouard Vermeulen has a business card money can't buy: he designs bespoke clothes for Princess Mathilde, the wife of the heir to the Belgian throne. His style is discreet, feminine and sexy. More affordable, off the peg clothing is available in his flagship store. *Rue de Namur 78 | www.natan.be | metro 2, 6: Porte de Namur*

STIJL (125 D3) (*m F2*)
An institution which boosted the status of rue Antoine Dansaert as a focus for fashion. Still in the vanguard for the latest Belgian styles. *Rue Antoine Dansaert 74 | metro: Bourse*

MUSIC

MUSICA NOVA (130 B1) (*m H4*)
Huge selection of traditional and contemporary music from Africa and the Caribbean. *Galerie d'Ixelles 24–28 | metro 2,6: Porte de Namur*

UNITED MUSIK (125 D4) (*m G3*)
Specialist shop selling old 45s, LPs and CDs, but also electro, free jazz, funk soul and reggae. *Place Fontainas 26 | metro: Anneessens*

Stijl – in the vanguard of Belgian fashion

UT PICTURA MUSICA ★ (125 F5) (*m G4*)
Specialist music shop of a rather unusual kind. Stocked here are small European classical labels with recordings by top musicians, including those by Belgium's most famous conductor Philippe Herreweghe on his own label, PHI. Something of a salon atmosphere; friendly, knowledgeable staff. Open Sunday, but closed Monday. *Rue Bodenbroek 8 (Grand Sablon) | www.outere-music.com | tram 92, 94: Petit Sablon*

JEWELLERY & ACCESSORIES

INSIDER TIP L'ANTICHAMBRE
(129 E5) (*ⅅ G8*)

Former top photographer Anne-Pascale Mathy-Devalck creates fragrances to personal specifications. She can even recreate that memorable perfume grandma used to wear. Allergen-free ingredients for allergy sufferers. *Place Georges Brugmann 13 | bus 60: Georges Brugmann*

LOW BUDGET

▶ In May/June and September/October Brussels is gripped by clearance fever. People are keen to sell off their odds and ends, including many real bargains, at the atmospheric *braderies*. See the *MAD* supplement of the daily newspaper *Le Soir* for full listings.

▶ Branded clothing from the previous season at *DOD* **(130 A3)** (*ⅅ H6*), look out for special deals in the soldes (sales) in July and January *(DOD Homme | rue du Bailli 81–85 | DOD Femme | rue du Bailli 64 | DOD Kids | rue du Bailli 8).*

▶ Inexpensive tableware, room furnishings, gifts at the *Dishes Factory* (**(125 D2)** (*ⅅ F2*) | *quai-aux-Briques 58*). Cost of crockery calculated by the kilo (*la vaisselle au kilo*). **(125 E5)** (*ⅅ G4*) | *rue Haute 124–126*

▶ A great selection of second-hand CDs – with world music the speciality, also jazz and pop – at *Arlequin.* **(125 E4)** (*ⅅ G3*) | *rue de Chêne 7 | www.arlequin.net*

HOLEMANS (130 A2) (*ⅅ G5*)
They have been designing and producing jewellery here since 1922. Specialities include high-class engagement rings and avant-garde pendants and bracelets made of INSIDER TIP Orichalque, a patented alloy which expands or contracts depending on the ambient temperature or that of the body. *Av. Louise 71 (in the patio of the Conrad Hotel, place Wiltcher) | www.holemans.com | tram 92, 94: Stéphanie*

LORENZO LEBON (130 B2) (*ⅅ H5*)
Elegant, sporty handbags and travel bags with concealed brand name. The lining is printed with pictures of animal bones and similar. *Chaussee d'Ixelles 200 | www.lorenzolebon.com | bus 71: Fernand Cocq*

LILÙ (130 A3) (*ⅅ H6*)
Specialises in casual shoulder bags and classic, wire-free clutch bags in striking colours. *Rue du Bailli 9 | www.lilu.be | tram 94: Bailli*

MARIE LE LORRAIN (129 E5) (*ⅅ G8*)
Cool creations with fine hardwood, glass or synthetic beads, often using recycled jewellery. *Rue Berkendael 175 | tram 92: Molière*

LE SHOP DE CHRISTOPHE COPPENS
(125 D2) (*ⅅ F2*)

A wide range of daring hats, caps, scarves, belts, and recently ties and other accessories for men is leading to strong sales in Paris, New York, Tokyo and Shanghai. *Rue Léon Lepage 2 | metro: Bourse*

SUPERGREEN ME ☺
(125 D3) (*ⅅ F3*)

An esoteric range of goods, including beauty products, bed and bath linen, clothing for children and parents, home furnishings. There is, however, a unify-

Utterly delicious – the best butter biscuits in the world at Dandoy in rue au Beurre

ing factor – everything bears the eco-label. *Rue Van Artevelde 10 | www.super-greenme.be | metro: Bourse*

PÂTISSERIE & CONFISERIE

DANDOY ★ (125 E3) (*ω G3*)
The interior of this biscuiterie has hardly changed since 1826 when it was found-ed. The elegant ladies of Brussels and tourists from Japan come here to buy the best homemade butter biscuits in the world. Other specialities include *pain à la grecque*, a fine cinammon pastry with caster sugar, almond speculaas biscuits and the marzipan-filled *pavés de Brux-elles. Rue au Beurre 31 | metro: Bourse*

FABRICE COLLIGNON (130 B5) (*ω H7*)
Small *chocolaterie* with a *tearoom* in Brussels' fashionable quarter. Its speci-ality: pralines with a fruit jelly or herb fillings (basil, lavender and horseradish). *Chaussée de Waterloo 587 | tram 4, 23, 24: Bascule*

IRSI (130 A3) (*ω H6*)
For heavenly-tasting *manons*, thick pralines with a thick butter cream and alcohol filling. Another popular delicacy from this small, traditional confectionery is the *pâte de fruits* or fruit candy. *Rue du Bailli 15 | tram 94: Lesbroussart*

LAURENT GERBAUD ☺
(125 F4) (*ω G3*)
Fruit is best coated in the finest organic dark chocolate – **INSIDER TIP** completely sugar-free for diabetics. Unusual creative designs at Easter and Christmas. *Rue Ra-venstein 2 | www.chocolatsgerbaud.be | metro 1, 5: Gare Centrale*

MARCOLINI ★ ● ☺ (125 E5) (*ω G4*)
The Japanese design of Pierre Marco-lini's flagship store matches the perfect-ly formed pralines and their packaging. The *grand cru* chocolate is manufactured from select organic cocoa beans. A real classic are the *saveurs du monde*, mini-bars of dark chocolate. *Rue des Minimes 1 | tram 92, 94: Petit Sablon*

ENTERTAINMENT

CITY **WHERE TO START?**

The really hip congregate in the fashionable area around **rue Antoine Dansaert** and the clubs and discos by the **canal** are grow-ing in increasing popularity. Around **place du Luxembourg** and in **rue Ar-chimède** the expats largely tend to keep to themselves, but in the cafés and wine bars around **place Flagey, place du Châtelain** and **place Saint-Boniface** they mingle with the local bobos. The alternative scene around **parvis de Saint-Gilles** is lively, while the jeunesse dorée – young folk with money and an eye for fashion – head for **place Saint-Job**.

Brussels' nightlife is flourishing in the estaminets – the beer and wine bars – and cafés beside the bustling squares. At the other end of the scale devotees of the performing arts can look forward to a dance scene to rival New York's, professional theatres in abundance and also high-quality productions in one of the finest opera houses in the world.

The younger generation is spoilt for choice: jazz, chanson, pop, techno, world and much more, most of it in the fashionable quarter around *rue Antoine Dansaert* and alongside the canal. Later on in the evening, the party crowd con-gregates in the *Marolles quarter* and the districts of *Ixelles* and *Saint-Gilles*. Place du *Sablon* and the *Grand' Place* are the focal points for a rather mixed crowd of

Photo: The Marché aux Poissons, Brussels' famous fish market

Chanson, techno, ethno, jazz or opera – music matters in the multicultural metropolis

young and old, locals and tourists. The EU quarter is almost exclusively the domain of expatriates. Chanson and jazz concerts usually begin around 9pm; in the discos it is usually midnight before things start to liven up. Admission prices are about ten euros.

BARS & CAFÉS

L'ARCHIDUC (125 D2) *(Ø F2)*
Art Deco bar steeped in tradition, where jazz rules. Nat King Cole once played here. In-house DJs on Thursday, live jazz from 5pm to 7pm Sat and Sun. *Daily 4pm–5am | tel. 0 25 12 06 52 | rue Antoine Dansaert 6 | www.archiduc.net | metro 1: Sainte Catherine*

INSIDER TIP BAR DU MATIN
(129 D4) *(Ø F7)*
New and very fashionable meeting place near the Institut de Radioélectricité et de Cinématographie (INRACI), with an interior laid out in 1950s style. Vast terrace for the trendsetters with blankets provided

Kriek, lambic and gueuze – real ale from the on-site brewery at À la Mort Subite

when the weather gets cooler. In-house DJs at the weekend. *Daily 8am–2am | chaussée d'Alsemberg 172 | metro: Albert*

INSIDER TIP LE BAR À GILLES ●
(129 D2) (*ω F5–6*)
Cool meeting place for an apéritif with classics such as martini or port, but why not spoil yourself with a piscine, i.e. champagne on the rocks? Good selection of wines, tapas and daily specials. *Daily 11am–12.30am | parvis de Saint-Gilles 28 | metro: Parvis de Saint-Gilles*

BRASSERIE VERSCHUEREN
(129 D2) (*ω F5*)
Lively meeting place with an old-fashioned feel. *Daily 8am–2am | parvis de Saint-Gilles 11–13 | metro: Parvis de Saint-Gilles*

CAFÉ BELGA ★ (130 C3) (*ω J6*)
The place to be for the beau monde with intellectual aspirations. A good selection of newspapers to read as you enjoy your drink. But here you collect your order from the bar yourself. *Daily 9.30am–3am | place Flagey 18 | bus 71: Flagey*

LE CERCLE DES VOYAGEURS
(125 E4) (*ω G3*)
In a building dating from 1695, there's a distinctly colonial club feel. Heavy Chesterfield chairs, world music and subdued lighting. Ideal for a chat over an exquisite tea, wine or abbey beer. *Daily 11am–2 am | rue des Grands Carmes 18 | metro: Bourse*

CHEZ RICHARD (125 E5) (*ω G4*)
Tiny café much favoured by the Sablon crowd. Terrace. *Daily 7am–4am | rue des Minimes 2 | tram 92, 94: Petit Sablon*

CIRIO (125 E3) (*ω G3*)
Widows dressed to kill, quick-witted gentlemen of the road, intellectuals and students meet here in a Belle Époque setting. Authentic, unchanged in years, often quiet. *Daily 10am–3am | place de la Bourse 18 | metro: Bourse*

CRYSTAL LOUNGE ★ (125 F6) (*ω G5*)
Elegant, international-type bar with a breathtaking alabaster counter. Barman Raphael Trémérie has won many prestigious awards. Currently in demand: edible cocktails, i.e. creations in mousse and

jelly or the award-winning Perfect Louise (vodka, cream of banana, nectar of mango, passion fruit and lemon juice). *Daily 10am–1am | av. de la Toison d'Or 40 (in the Hotel Sofitel-Louise) | metro 2, 6: Louise*

DELECTA (130 C3) (*Ø J6*)
Rather offbeat wine bar near fashionable place Flagey. The rich and beautiful assemble here on Thursday for INSIDERTIP aperitifs and top DJs. *Mon–Fri 10am–1am | rue Lannoy 2 | tram 94: Vleurga*

FLORIS BAR (125 E3) (*Ø G3*)
More than 2,000 different high-octane spirits, mainly gin and vodka, but also INSIDERTIP absinthe, the fiendishly-strong tipple of the Belle Époque imbibers. *Wed–Sat 8pm–6am | impasse de la Fidélité 12 | metro: De Brouckère*

À LA MORT SUBITE (125 F3) (*Ø G2–3*)
Jacques Brel and Maurice Béjart used to be regulars at the 'sudden death' brasserie. Today in what is a listed Belle Époque interior, actors, students and tourists enjoy *gueuze* and *kriek* from the on-site brewery. *Daily 10am–1am | rue Montagne-aux-Herbes-Potagères 7 | metro: De Brouckère*

PARC SAVOY (131 E6) (*Ø O*)
An old villa transformed into a chic apartment. Thirty-somethings, including many expats, meet here for lively discussions and house music. Smart restaurant. *Thu–Sat 7pm–4am | place Marie-José 9 | tram 94: Marie-José*

INSIDERTIP PIXEL (125 E5) (*Ø G4*)
A highly-original setting. Leading Brussels designer, Charles Kaisin, enlarged the 5400 pixels from a photo and printed them on to cushions of synthetic material. Call in here after a walk in place du Sablon. Fine wines and equally fine nibbles. *Daily 10am–10pm | rue Ernest Allard 39–41 | tram 92, 94: Poelaert*

ROXI (130 A3) (*Ø H6*)
Brick, stainless steel, glass and red leather combine to create the unusual ambience in this fashionable meeting place in the trendy Châtelain quarter. Innovative cocktails and meals. Regular live concerts. *Daily 8am–1am | rue du Bailli 82 | tram 94: Bailli*

L'ULTIME ATOME (130 B1) (*Ø H5*)
Cool meeting place for students, artists and yuppies in a square that is growing in popularity. Nourishing snacks. *Daily 9am–1am | rue Saint-Boniface 14 | metro 2, 6: Porte de Namur*

MARCO POLO HIGHLIGHTS

★ **Café Belga**
A popular haunt of the jeunesse dorée → p. 76

★ **Crystal Lounge**
Amazing cocktails in elegant surroundings→ p. 76

★ **Espace Magh**
World music in the Maghreb cultural centre → p. 78

★ **Le Fuse**
One of the hottest discos → p. 78

★ **Théâtre Royal de la Monnaie**
World class musical experiences → p. 80

★ **Recyclart**
Exciting crossover experiments in an old railway station → p. 78

★ **Palais des Beaux-Arts**
World-class concerts in an Art Nouveau palace → p. 80

THE BEER FACTORY (126 C5) (*J4*)
Another fashionable bar, this one belonging to the Haacht family brewing dynasty. The bar counter fits inside in an opened copper mash tun, nice seating areas with armchairs in the gallery. Also abbey beers. EU clientele. *Mon–Fri 10am–midnight | place du Luxembourg 6 | metro 2, 6: Trône*

ZEBRA BAR (125 D3) (*F3*)
Bar with a 'deconstructivist' interior on

Recyclart – a former railway station that is now a crossover hotspot

place Saint-Géry, popular spot to meet up, offbeat setting. When the weather is fine, sit outside on the spacious terrace and enjoy a delicious sandwich. *Daily 10am–4pm | place Saint-Géry 33–35 | metro: Bourse*

CHANSON, POP & WORLD

ANCIENNE BELGIQUE (125 E3) (*F3*)
Every evening pop, rock and crossover concerts by stars who have not yet made it to the big stage. Experimental music. *Bd. Anspach 110 | tel. 0 25 48 24 24 | www.abconcerts.be | metro: Bourse*

LE BOTANIQUE (126 B2) (*H2*)
The best chansonniers and new talent in a nice setting. *Rue Royale 236 | tel. 0 22 18 37 32 | www.botanique.be | metro 2: Botanique*

LE CABARET AUX CHANSONS (125 E4) (*G3*)
Talented performers of chanson, ethno and world perform in this no-nonsense Brussels club. *Marché aux Fromages 22B | tel. 0 25 12 51 92 | www.cabaretauxchansons.be | metro: Bourse, Gare Centrale*

ESPACE MAGH ★ (125 D4) (*F3*)
Top musicians from the Middle East, the Caribbean and Africa. Crossover and underground. *Rue du Poinçon 173 | tel. 0 22 74 05 10 | www.espacemagh.be | metro: Anneessens*

RECYCLART ★ (125 D–E5) (*F4*)
Brussels hotspot for everything else, genres that cannot be neatly categorised. The setting, a former railway station, was designed by graffiti artists. Alternative clientele, art students and bobos, who also appreciate the bar. *Rue des Ursulines 25 | tel. 0 25 02 57 34 | metro: Anneessens*

DISCOTHEQUES

LE FUSE ★ (125 D6) (*F5*)
Old cinema that is now the place for hot techno, mixed by top DJs. The earlier in the morning, the more relaxed the atmosphere, theme nights, alternative clientele. *Open from Sat 10pm | rue Blaes 206 | metro 2, 6: Porte de Hal*

LES JEUX D'HIVER (130 C6) (*⌘ J8*)
The city's smart set meets at this exclusive disco in the Bois de la Cambre to dance to fusion music. *Thu–Sat, bar from 9pm, disco 12.30am–7am | chemin du Croquet 1 | tram 94: Legrand*

K-NAL (123 E6) (*⌘ F1*)
In a timber avant-garde building by the canal. Cool disco evenings, live bands, parties. *Av. du Port 1 | tel. 0 23 74 87 38 | www.k-nal.be | metro 2, 6: Yser*

LE MIRANO CONTINENTAL (126 C3) (*⌘ J2*)
Converted cinema with chrome and glitter. This is where the city's best-looking girls and boys come to dance – or at least that's what they say. You've got to have something to get past the doormen though. *Sat 11pm–5am | chaussée de Louvain | metro 2, 6: Madou*

THE FLAT (126 A5) (*⌘ H4*)
Subtle electro music, small dance floor; on the first floor the club is decked out

like an apartment and you can even have your drinks in the bathroom. Drink prices subject to demand. Many expats. *Wed–Sat 6pm–2am | rue de la Reinette 12 | metro 2, 6: Porte de Namur*

JAZZ

JAZZ STATION (127 F2) (*⌘ L2*)
Several promoters of jazz concerts have moved into an old station. Varied programme, workshops, nice café. *Wed–Sat, café 11am–6pm, concerts 8.30pm | chaussée de Louvain 193A | tel. 0 27 33 13 78 | www.jazzstation.be | tram 25: Meiser*

MUSIC VILLAGE (125 E3) (*⌘ F3*)
Upmarket jazz club with the emphasis on blues. *Wed–Sat 7pm | rue des Pierres 50 | tel. 0 25 13 13 45 | www.themusicvillage.com | metro: Bourse*

INSIDER TIP **SAZZ 'N JAZZ** (126 B1) (*⌘ H1*)
Club in a wonderful townhouse serving Mediterranean cuisine. Crossover be-

FOOTBALL IN BRUSSELS – A CITY DIVIDED BY COLOUR

Brussels has two top-class football teams and many of their players represent the national side, the *diables rouges. Royal Sporting Club Anderlecht RSCA*, founded in 1908, are known as the *les Mauves, mauve et blanc* or *mauves army* after their shirt colours. The 30-time Belgian champions have accumulated by far the most titles in the national league and have a broad fan base. One of their stars from the past was Paul van Himst, who made a record 457 appearances for the club. Home games take place in the *Stade*

Constant Vanden Stock (Parc Astrid | (129 F1) (⌘ A5) av. Théo Verbeecklaan 2 | www.rsca.be | Metro 5: Saint-Guidon).
But their deadly rivals since 1936 have been *RWDM Molenbeek*, who in 2004 changed their name to *FC Brussels*. Les rouge et noir have produced football legends such as Wesley Sonck, Franky van der Elst, Franky Vercauteren and Marc Wuyts. Home games are staged at the *Stade Edmond Machtens | (129 F1) (⌘ B1–2) rue Charles Malis 61 | www.fc-brussels.be | bus 49: Leroy*.

tween blues, soul, free jazz and world music. Young multicultural clientele. *Wed–Sat 7pm–midnight | rue Royale 241 | www.sazznjazz.be | tram 94: Gillon*

SOUNDS (130 B1) (📖 H5)

Small jazz café with a varied programme from Aka Moon to the stars of tomorrow. *Daily 8pm | rue de la Tulipe 28 | tel. 0 25 12 92 50 | metro: Porte de Namur | bus 71: Fernand Cocq*

CINEMA

Cinematek (125 F4) (📖 G–H3)

For movie fans: huge archive, several performances daily, theme-orientated. Intimate screening room. *Rue Baron Horta 9 | tel. 0 25 07 83 70 | www.cinematheque.be | metro 1, 5: Gare Centrale*

NOVA (125 F3) (📖 G3)

Cinema specialising in underground productions, **INSIDER TIP** offbeat café. *Rue d'Arenberg 3 | tel. 0 25 11 24 77 | www.nova-cinema.com | metro: De Brouckère*

LOW BUDGET

▶ *Arsène50* sells tickets at half-price for same-day performances in over 100 theatres and venues *(Tue–Sat 12.30pm–5.30 pm) | Cinéma Arenberg |* **(125 F3)** *(📖 G3) | Galerie de la Reine 26 and Flagey |* **(130 C3)** *(📖 J6) | place Sainte-Croix).*

▶ The ● Grand' Place is a venue for free chanson, jazz, pop and rock concerts, especially in summer and December. Performances often broadcast on big screens. *visitbrussels.be*

CLASSICAL & OPERA

CONSERVATOIRE ROYAL (125 F5) (📖 G4)

Chamber concerts with renowned international stars and appearances by younger Belgian talent. ● Regular free concerts by students. *Rue de la Régence 30 | tel. 0 25 11 04 27 | www.conservatoire.be, www.kcb.be | tram 92, 94: Petit Sablon*

FLAGEY (130 C3) (📖 J6)

Music from classical to world in this Art Deco setting. Excellent accoustics. *Place Flagey | tel. 0 26 27 16 40 | www.flagey.be | bus 71: Flagey*

PALAIS DES BEAUX-ARTS ★
(125 F4) (📖 G–H3)

The large, oval-shaped concert hall in Victor Horta's Art Deco masterpiece ranks among the best in the world. Where celebrated Belgian orchestras and soloists give guest performances. Younger musicians showcase their talents in the smaller halls. *Rue Ravenstein 23 | tel. 0 25 07 84 44 | www.bozar.be | metro 1, 5: Gare Centrale*

THÉÂTRE ROYAL DE LA MONNAIE ★
(125 E3) (📖 G2)

World class musical events staged in an opera house dating back over 300 years, plus ultra-modern workshops, studio productions, symphony concerts, lieder evenings, ballet and dance. To get a flavour, check listings for chamber concerts by orchestral musicians in the Grand Foyer at a much reduced rate. *Place de la Monnaie | tel. (*) 070 23 39 39 | www.lamonnaie.be | metro: De Brouckère*

CASINO

VIAGE (125 E3) (📖 G2)

Some 126 gaming tables for roulette, blackjack, stud poker and punto banco, plus 250 gaming machines. Good restaurant, panoramic view from the rooftop terraces. Dress code: smart-casual. Minimum age for admission: 21. Identification essential. *Daily noon–5 am | Admission free | tel. (*) 070 23 39 39 | www. viage.be | boulevard Anspach 30 | metro: De Brouckère*

DANCE, THEATRE & CIRCUS

CHAPELLE DES BRIGITTINES (125 D5) (*Ⅲ F4*)

Between unplastered walls, experimental dance productions and performances by young choreographers. Festival at the end of August/early September. *Petite rue des Brigittines 1 | tel. 0 25 06 43 00 | www.brigittines.be | bus 48: Chapelley*

ESPACE CATASTROPHE (129 E4) (*Ⅲ G7*)

Young avant-garde circus artists perform in an old ice factory. Great atmosphere. *Rue de la Glacière 18 | tel. 0 25 38 12 02 | www. catastrophe.be | bus 29: Plasky*

INSIDER TIP ESAC (O) (*Ⅲ O*)

The Brussels School of Circus Arts ranks among the best in the world. Every year on certain dates in March, June and December, students display their talents in the school's beautiful Art Nouveau salon. Reservations are essential as many visitors with a professional interest will be in attendance. *Rue Williame | tel. 0 26 75 68 84 | www.esac.be | metro 5: Hermann-Debroux*

HALLES DE SCHAERBEEK (126 B1) (*Ⅲ J1*)

International avant-garde circus groups perform in the impressive market halls. Plus experimental dance, theatre and new music. *Royale-Sainte-Marie 22 | tel. 0 22 18 21 07 | www.halles.be | tram 92, 94: Sainte-Marie*

KAAITHEATER (123 E6) (*Ⅲ F1*)

The theatre on the canal is mainly the preserve of the more established leading Flemish directors and choreographers, also new music. Nice café (open 11am).

Théâtre Royal de la Monnaie – for world-class musical events

Square Saincteletette 18 | tel. 0 24 27 87 72 | www.kaaitheater.be | metro 2, 6: Yser

THÉÂTRE NATIONAL (125 E2) (*Ⅲ G2*)

Belgium's best theatre. Classical repertoire and experimental theatre from all over the world, with work of the highest quality guaranteed. *Boulevard Emile Jacqumain 111–115 | tel. 0 22 03 41 11 | www. theatrenational.be | metro: De Brouckère*

WHERE TO STAY

Every day, conferences, congresses and conventions draw visitors to Brussels. It's the headquarters of the European Union, NATO and countless other international organisations and as a result many luxury, and usually very expensive, hotels have established themselves in the city to cater for the needs of the corporate traveller.

The majority of hotels do indeed offer modern comforts, but in the rather bland style typical of the global companies running them. Not that long ago there was a shortage of small, good-quality family hotels and bed and breakfasts in Brussels, but with the increase in cultural tourism there has been a corresponding growth in boutique-style accommodation. At weekends and in August, at Easter and at Christmas, when the international conference merry-go-round comes to a halt, many of the top hotels offer discounts of up to 50%.

HOTELS: EXPENSIVE

BE MANOS ⭐ (124 C5) (*⃝ E4*)
This glamorous, boutique hotel in black, white and silver is situated between Bruxelles-Midi railway station (the stop for Thalys, ICE, TGV and Eurostar) and the city centre. Facilities include luxurious bathrooms and a spa zone in Chinese slate, elegant lounges and a beautiful rooftop terrace to relax on. Friendly service from a hands-on proprietor. Breakfast with organic produce. *60 rooms | square de l'Aviation 23 | tel. 02 5 20 65 65 | www. bemanos.com | metro: Lemonnier*

Photo: Hotel Amigo

There's always the mainstream chains, but the choice now also includes a growing number of stylish and distinctive hotels

LE DIXSEPTIÈME ★ (125 E4) *(∅ G3)*

This listed building with Baroque hall, stairs and lounges, as well as rooms furnished with timeless elegance, is only a stone's throw from the Grand' Place. *24 rooms | rue de la Madeleine 25 | tel. 0 25 17 17 17 | www.ledixseptieme.be | metro 1, 5: Gare Centrale*

DOLCE LA HULPE ● (133 D3) *(∅ O)*

This hotel is situated a few kilometres outside the town in the middle of woodland. The rooms are spacious and facilities include two bars, two restaurants, two tennis courts, in-house mountain bikes for hire, golf and riding nearby. The main attraction is the luxury INSIDER TIP Spa Cinq Mondes with pool, sauna, Turkish bath, fitness suite, as well as a variety of massage and beauty treatments. Open to non-patrons, too (whole day programme from 175 euros). *264 rooms | chaussée de Bruxelles 135, 1310 La Hulpe | tel. 0 22 90 98 00 | www.dolce-la-hulpe-brussels-hotel.com | TEC-bus 366 (dep. place Flagey): La Hulpe IBM*

Glitz and glamour in the lobby of the Métropole

MÉTROPOLE ★ (125 E3) (*M G2*)

Albert Einstein and Sarah Bernhardt, Marie Curie and Charles de Gaulle, as well as many other celebrities from the world of politics, science and culture, have stayed here in the course of the last hundred years or so. The lobby, lounges and restaurant are dazzlingly ornate, the rooms are comfortably furnished in a contemporary style. Cocktail bar and terraced café are very popular haunts among wealthier city folk. *298 rooms | place de Brouckère 31 | tel. 0 22 17 23 00 | www.metropolehotel.be | metro: De Brouckère*

PARK (127 F5) (*M L4*)

Modern comforts in an elegant town house by the Parc du Cinquantenaire, an ideal location for joggers and walkers. Plus a private garden, fitness suite, sauna and jacuzzi. Excellent value for money. *53 rooms | av. de l'Yser 21 | tel. 0 27 35 74 00 | www.parkhotelbrussels. be | metro 1, 5: Mérode*

ROYAL WINDSOR HOTEL
(125 E4) (*M G3*)

Classy establishment in the city centre with twelve rooms designed by top **INSIDER TIP** Brussels fashion designers, such as Jean-Paul Knott and Marina Yee. The view from the latter's avant-garde suite includes the impressive town hall. *266 rooms | rue Duquesnoy 5 | tel. 0 25 05 55 55 | www.royalwindsorbrussels. com | metro 1, 5: Gare Centrale*

THE DOMINICAN (125 E3) (*M G2*)

Built in a style that recalls its former function as a monastery, this hotel is situated behind the opera house. Spacious rooms elegantly-furnished with luxurious bathrooms. The lounges with open fires and candlelight make it a popular spot for afternoon tea, apéritifs and drinks after the opera. *150 rooms | rue Léopold 9 | tel. 0 22 03 08 08 | www.thedominican.be | metro: De Brouckère*

WARWICK BARSEY HOTEL
(130 C5) (*M J7*)

In an extravagantly designed building located in the elegant part of avenue Louise in close proximity to several parks. There is a fitness suite, gourmet restaurant with bar, large terrace and the hotel has its own garage. *99 rooms | av. Louise 381–383 | tel. 0 26 49 98 00 | www.warwickbarsey.com | tram 94: Abbaye*

HOTELS: MODERATE

AGENDA LOUISE (129 F3) (*Ø G6*)

This friendly establishment is located in a quiet side street off elegant avenue Louise. *38 rooms | rue de Florence 6–8 | tel. 0 25 39 00 31 | www.hotel-agenda.com | tram 92, 94: Stéphanie*

ARLEQUIN (125 E3) (*Ø G3*)

A pretty hotel with friendly staff situated between the Galeries Saint-Hubert and the opera house. Breakfast is served on the glazed rooftop terrace. Fitness suite. *92 rooms. | rue de la Fourche 17–19 | tel. 0 25 14 16 15 | www.arlequin.be | metro: Bourse*

AUBERGE DU REPOS DES CHASSEURS ★ (O) (*Ø O*)

The proprietors of a restaurant renowned for its game specialities have adapted the old building to create eleven pretty guest rooms. For total peace and tranquillity on the edge of the Forêt de Soignes. *Av. Charles-Albert 11 | tel. 0 26 60 46 72 | www.repos-des-chasseurs. com | tram 94: Fauconnerie*

BLOOM! ★ (126 B2) (*Ø H1*)

Cool and stylish hotel is beside the old botanical gardens. A fresco by a young European artist adorns every room. Smart lounges and restaurants, and a fitness suite with panoramic view; a hearty breakfast with organically-sourced products; DJs at the weekend and regular art exhibitions. *305 rooms | rue Royale 250 | tel. 0 22 20 66 11 | www.hotelbloom.be | metro 2, 6, Tram 92, 94: Botanique*

HOTEL CAFÉ PACIFIC ★

(125 E3) (*Ø F2*)

This intimate, stylish and very comfortable establishment with an Art Deco café is situated in the heart of the fashion quarter around rue Antoine Dansaert. *12 rooms | rue Antoine Dansaert 57 | tel. 0 22 13 00 80 | www.hotelcafepacific. com | metro: Bourse*

CHAMBORD (126 A5) (*Ø H4*)

Although it occupies a fine location in the exclusive shopping area of the Upper Town, this hotel still boasts a quiet location. Rooms are elegantly furnished (some with patio and fine view). Nice bar and breakfast room in the airy glazed bay window. *70 rooms | rue de Namur 82 | tel. 0 25 48 99 10 | www.hotel-chambord.be | metro 2, 6: Porte de Namur*

DES COLONIES (125 F1) (*Ø G1*)

This Art Deco hotel has a broad lobby decorated with a mural of the US army who were billeted here in 1944. Fully

---

MARCO POLO HIGHLIGHTS

★ **Be Manos**
Smart boutique hotel with spa and fitness centre → p. 82

★ **Métropole**
Brussels' most recent 100-year-old palace → p. 84

★ **Auberge du Repos des Chasseurs**
Peaceful country retreat → p. 85

★ **Hotel Café Pacific**
Luxury and style in the fashion designers' quarter → p. 85

★ **Bloom!**
Cool atmosphere, modern art and DJs → p. 85

★ **Le Dixseptième**
Baroque residence behind the Grand' Place → p. 83

renovated in 2001, comfortable rooms in a quiet location. Friendly service. *96 rooms | rue des Croisades 6–10 | tel. 0 22 05 16 00 | www.hotel-des-colonies.be | metro: Rogier*

LE SABLON (125 E5) (*W G4*)

An attractively-furnished hotel with a nice location in a quiet side street off stylish place du Sablon. Sauna. *32 rooms | rue de la Paille 2–8 | tel. 0 25 13 60 40 | www.eurostarssablon.com | tram 92, 94: Petit Sablon*

INSIDER TIP ▶ THE VINTAGE
(129 E1) (*W G5*)

This hotel is ideally situated in close proximity to place Louise with rooms in the style of the 1950s, 1960s and 1970s. Some examples of the elegant furnishings, such as chairs, lamps, vases and carpets, are available for sale. It boasts a

LUXURY HOTELS

Amigo (125 E4) (*W G3*)

In an exclusive location behind the Hôtel de Ville, furnished in discreet elegance with carefully-selected antiques. The rooms and bathrooms are spacious. There is a modern fitness centre, and the hotel has its own garage and Boccon, a first-class Italian restaurant. *174 rooms | double rooms from 640 euros | rue de l'Amigo 1–3 | tel. 0 25 47 47 47 | www.roccofortecollection.com | metro: Bourse*

Conrad (130 A2) (*W G5*)

US presidents and Arab sheikhs, steel and shipping magnates have all stayed here. Hidden away behind the Belle Époque facade is the epitome of modern-day luxury. Ballrooms to rival the Palais Royal, a restaurant and Brussels' finest fitness centre spread over three storeys. *254 rooms | double rooms from 725 euros | av. Louise 71 | tel. 0 25 42 42 42 | www.conradhotels.com | tram 92, 94: Stéphanie*

Manos Ier (129 E3) (*W G6*)

Extravagant splendour in an old town house in the smart Upper Town, this hotel boasts spacious lounges and rooms with Rococo furniture, gilded mirrors and marble baths. There's a beautiful garden and the Kolya, a fashionable restaurant. Own garage. *50 rooms | double rooms from 350 euros | chaussée de Charleroi 100–106 | tel. 0 25 37 96 82 | www.manoshotel.com | tram 92: Faider*

Stanhope (126 B5) (*W H4*)

This is a home fit for an English lord, with a breath of the countryside in Brussels' most expensive banking quarter. Fine garden and service you can only dream about. *108 rooms | double rooms from 425 euros | rue du Commerce 9 | tel. 0 25 06 91 11 | www.stanhope.be | Metro 2, 6: Trône*

The Hotel ☆ (126 A6) (*W G4*)

It is not just British pop stars, Israeli prime ministers, American businessmen and Japanese bankers who adore this hotel; distinguished guests from all over Europe choose it too. Panoramic view over Brussels, plus a Michelin-starred restaurant. *433 rooms | double rooms from 320 euros | bd. de Waterloo 38 | tel. 0 25 04 33 35 | www.thehotel.be | metro 2, 6: Louise*

Arab sheikhs and US presidents swim in the 17-m long (55ft) pool at the Conrad

well-stocked wine bar in a pretty interior courtyard. *29 rooms | rue Dejoncker 45 | tel. 0 25 33 99 80 | www.vintagehotel.be | metro 2, 6, tram 92, 94: Louise*

WELCOME (125 E2) (*Ø F2*)
A lovely hotel by the fish market with 15 individually-designed rooms. *Rue du Peuplier 1 | tel. 0 22 19 95 46 | www.hotelwelcomecom | metro 1, 5: Sainte-Catherine*

INSIDER TIP THE WHITE HOTEL (130 B3) (*Ø H6*)
Located close to the smart quarter around place du Châtelain and place Flagey, this hotel has very large, white rooms with selected designer furniture, some with their own patio and panoramic view. Facilities include computer booths, breakfast with organic produce; it even has its own electric bikes for hire (18 euros per day). *53 rooms | av. Louise 212 | tel. 0 26 44 29 29 | www.thewhitehotel.be | tram 81, 94: Bailli*

HOTELS: BUDGET

ATLAS (125 D3) (*Ø F2*)
This comfortable hotel is centrally situated on a quiet square in the fashionable area around rue Antoine Dansaert. Take breakfast with a view of the town wall. Good service. *93 rooms | rue du Vieux-Marché-aux-Grains 30–34 | tel. 0 25 02 60 06 | www.atlas-hotel.be | metro: Bourse*

BEVERLY HILLS HOTEL (129 F1) (*Ø H5*)
A very comfortable, post-modern-style establishment in the elegant shopping area. Good fitness suite, plus sauna and jacuzzi. *33 rooms | rue du Prince Royal 71 | tel. 0 25 13 22 22 | www.hotelbeverlyhills.be | metro 2, 6: Louise*

DU CONGRÈS (126 B3) (*Ø H2*)
There is a warm and friendly Brussels atmosphere in these four fully-renovated town houses dating from the 19th century. Academics among the regulars. *61 rooms | rue du Congrès 42 | tel. 0 22 17 18 90 | www.hotelducongres.be | metro 2, 6: Madou*

DERBY (127 F5) (*Ø M4*)
A nice hotel with simple rooms situated only a short distance from the Parc du Cinquantenaire. *27 rooms | av. de Tervueren 24 | tel. 0 27 33 08 19 | www.hotelderby.be | metro 1, 5: Merode*

Cheap and cheerful –
the Sleep Well hostel

HOTEL GALIA (125 D6) (*F4*)

Overlooks the flea market. Ideal for early risers and admirers of the Bohemian lifestyle, very much part of the charm of the Marolles quarter. *24 rooms | place du Jeu de Balle | tel. 0 25 02 42 43 | www.hotel galia.com | Bus 48: Jeu de Balle*

GEORGE V (124 C3) (*F3*)

Close to the fashionable area around rue Antoine Dansaert, this family-friendly hotel is tastefully furnished. *16 rooms | rue 't Kint 23 | tel. 0 25 13 50 93 | www.hotel george5.com | metro: Anneessens*

À LA GRANDE CLOCHE (125 D4–5) (*F3*)

One of the last of the old style hotels – unpretentious, but very good value for money. Opposite that temple to gastronomy *Comme chez Soi. 37 rooms | place Rouppe 10–12 | tel. 0 25 12 61 40 | www.hotelgrande cloche.com | metro: Anneessens*

LA LÉGENDE (125 E4) (*F3*)

A nice, unpretentious family hotel situated near the Grand' Place and the Manneken Pis. *26 rooms | rue du Lombard 36 | tel. 0 25 12 82 90 | www.hotella legende.com | metro: Bourse*

NOGA (125 E2) (*F2*)

This friendly hotel with pretty rooms is situated between the fish market and the Baroque church of Saint-Jean-Baptiste au Béguinage, a quiet, secluded spot in the centre of the city. *19 rooms | rue du Béguinage 38 | tel. 0 22 18 67 63 | www.nogahotel.com | metro 1, 5: Sainte-Catherine*

PANTONE HOTEL (129 E2) (*G5*)

All the walls in this hotel are painted in distinctive colours, the rooms and bathrooms furnished in a minimalist style. There are two suites on the 8th floor with large terraces and a 🔆 panoramic view. The lounge is rather cramped; breakfast costs extra (15 euros). **INSIDER TIP** Boutique with chic designer articles. *61 rooms | place Loix 1 | tel. 0 25 41 48 98 | www.pantonehotel.com | metro 2, 6: Louise*

SAINT MICHEL (125 E4) (*G3*)

Four rooms with a view of the Grand' Place. A splendid place to stay, but unfortunately rather noisy. *15 rooms | Grand' Place 15 | tel. 0 25 11 09 56 | metro: Bourse*

APARTHOTELS

CITADINES APARTHOTELS (125 D2) (*F2*)

This modern building with a nice terrace is situated at the fish market, only minutes away from the Grand' Place, the opera house and the fashionable area around rue Antoine Dansaert. *169 rooms and apartments (from 66 euros) |*

quai au Bois à Brûler 51 | tel. 0 22 211411 | www.citadines.com | metro 1, 5: Sainte-Catherine

IMMOBE APARTHOTELS
(130 B–C5) (*ØØ H–J 7–8*)
In total there are 29 'residences', from a single room to the whole house, on elegant avenue Louise and side streets. From 52 euros per night, from 818 euros per month. *Av. Louise 331 | tel. 0 26 26 07 76 | www.immobe.be*

BED & BREAKFAST

The accommodation booking agency Bed & Brussels *(tel. 0 26 46 07 37 | www.bnb-brussels.be)* represents more than 350 establishments. The website has photos of all rooms, with selection according to quarter, proximity to museums etc. Prices usually in the 75–90 euro range.

CHAMBRES EN VILLE (126 B6) (*ØØ H4*)
This former mirror factory near the EU was furnished by a painter and art collector with souvenirs picked up on his travels. *5 rooms (90 euros) | rue de Londres 19 | tel. 0 25 12 92 90 | www.chambres enville.be | metro 2, 6: Trône*

INSIDERTIP THE LITTLE MAPLES
(131 E2) (*ØØ L5*)
Confectioner Marc Lindekens furnished the B & B, located not far from the EU quarter, in Bauhaus style to match the architecture. In the afternoon he serves pralines, chocolate and, in summer, home-made ice cream. *3 rooms (90–110 euros, incl. lunch and afternoon tea) | rue des Erables 26 | tel. 0 27 34 94 00 | www. littlemaples.com | tram 81: Chasse*

VAUDEVILLE (125 E3) (*ØØ G3*)
These elegant rooms are above the restaurant of the same name (10% price discount for residents) in the chic Galeries Saint-Hubert. Central location. *4 rooms (150 euros) | galerie de la Reine 11 | tel. 0 25 12 84 58 | www.chambresdhotesduvaudeville.be | metro: Bourse, Gare Centrale*

FOR YOUNG PEOPLE

AUBERGE BRUEGEL (125 E5) (*ØØ G4*)
This modern youth hostel is situated in the shadow of the Gothic Notre-Dame de la Chapelle between Marolles, Sablon and the Grand' Place. There's a bar, and an overnight stay starts at 19.50 euros. *135 beds | rue du Saint-Esprit 2 | tel. 0 25 11 04 36 | www.vjh.be | metro 1, 5: Gare Centrale*

CENTRE VINCENT VAN GOGH
(126 B2) (*ØØ H2*)
A large, independent youth hostel with prices ranging from 19 to 34 euros for a one-bed room to a ten-bed room. Bar, billiards, television/ video room. *210 beds | rue Traversière 8 | tel. 0 22 17 01 58 | www.chab.be | metro 2, 6: Botanique*

LOW BUDGET

▶ *Sleep Well*, a modern hostel in the city centre, with no upper age limit or curfew. There is a bar and regular live music. *42 twin rooms from 30 euros* | **(125 E2) (*ØØ G2*)** *rue du Damier 23 | tel. 0 22 18 50 50 | www. sleepwell.be | metro: Rogier*

▶ *Taxi Stop* runs an online home exchange service. You swap your house or apartment with a home owner in Belgium. *Rue Thérésienne 7 a/c | B-1000 Bruxelles | tel. (*) 0 70 22 22 92 | www.taxistop.be*

WALKING TOURS

The tours are marked in green in the street atlas,
the pull-out map and on the back cover

1 FROM THE MIDDLE AGES TO HIGH FASHION

It was from a 'house in the marsh' on the Grande-Île that Brussels, with all its contrasts, emerged. You can explore the area in two hours, but add in a little shopping and a couple of coffee breaks in the chic cafés, and it could easily take four hours.

Beside the Bourse → p. 28 in rue de la Bourse, you can peep through a glass roof at the excavated remains of the Old Town, which are on display in a museum known as Bruxella 1238 (*guided tours on the first Wednesday of the month at 11.15am and 3pm | pre-booking tel. 0 22 79 43 50 | admission 3 euros |* *www.bruxelles.be*). On the other side of boulevard Anspach, rue Jules van Praet leads to the place Saint-Géry → p. 32, a part of town popular for its fashionable cafés. In what was formerly the covered market, the splashing waters from an imposing fountain provide a focal point. Exhibitions are regularly staged here to highlight issues around the conservation of historic monuments and urban planning. Opposite the rear of the building the courtyard of the old housing complex leads to INSIDER TIP the only place where you can still see what is left of the River Senne. The reflection of the Baroque No-tre-Dame aux Riches Claires is captured romantically in the water.

Cross rue Saint-Christophe to rue des Chartreux. The facades of the watch-

Photo: Place Saint-Géry

Art Nouveau and green spaces – take a stroll around the Grande-Île, the university quarter, and the European Parliament

makers, An-Hor (no. 3) and Atelier Demarteau (no. 42), come straight out of a picturebook. Greenwich (no. 7) was where the artist René Magritte came to play chess. Rue des Chartreux leads to the smart place du Jardin aux Fleurs. In the rue Antoine Dansaert → p. 66 boutiques selling the latest fashions are sure to detain you and you will not get away with simply window-shopping. The top store here is Stijl → p. 71. At no. 81 your eyes will be drawn to the Art Deco gable. A detour through the shadowy rue Léon Lepage conveys a Parisian feel, whereas in rue du Rempart des Moines, behind the Baroque gateway near no. 21, an ancient fragment of Brussels life is revealed: rue de la Cigogne. Rue Antoine Dansaert now leads through to Porte de Flandre. Its rather down-to-earth features give way to lively cafés, galleries, boutiques and attic flats with fine views over the canal. Pass through the fashionable rue de Flandre (look behind no. 46 for a glimpse of the glorious Baroque facade of the Maison Bellone) and as far as place Sainte-Catherine → p. 32. A slight detour into rue Sainte-Catherine and you will soon find yourself in Brussels' Chinatown with its Oriental supermarkets and snack bars. In the square is the neo-Gothic church of Sainte-Catherine, where the faithful come to worship a small Black Madonna. All that remains of the original shrine is the Baroque Tour de la Vierge-Noire. Behind the chancel the Black Tower merges with a hotel facade, one of the few remaining sections of the original town wall dating from the 13th century. To the northern side of place Sainte-Catherine, long quays overlook rectangular strips of water, formerly the city's docks. Rue du Peuplier draws you on to the church of Saint-Jean-Baptiste au Béguinage → p. 33. Outside the portal of the classical Hospice Pachéco, a pretty tree-lined square opens up, beckoning you in to sit and relax for a few moments.

Rue de l'Hospice leads to rue de Laeken. Situated behind the heavy, black portal at no. 79 are three spectacular monuments to freemasonry. At the Musée belge de la Francmaçonnerie in no. 73 you are invited to step inside for a rare opportunity to learn more about the mysterious world of freemasonry and the importance of this often secret organisation to the city of Brussels. *(Sept–June Tue–Fri 1pm–5pm, Sat 1pm–4pm, July/Aug Tue–Sat 1pm–4pm, Thu guided visits by appointment | admission 6 euros | www.museummacionicum.be)*. In rue de Laeken some 99 young Brussels designers regularly stage exhibitions on behalf of Designed in Brussels *(www. designedinbrussels.be)*. No. 140 is the address of the neo-Renaissance style Koninklijke Vlaamse Schouwburg, the city's main Flemish theatre (1887) *(www. kvs.be)*.

2 STUDENT LIFE AND THE TRANQUILLITY OF THE CEMETERY

Half a day in the University Quarter and you will uncover numerous surprises. You will pass Art Deco buildings and monuments, cool cafés and the foreign embassies, terminating your walk at a cemetery, the last resting place of a number of celebrities with links to Brussels.

A good introduction is the Musée d'Ixelles. Well-heeled donors are to this very day filling the galleries of an erstwhile slaughterhouse with masterpieces of Belgian Symbolism, Expressionism and Surrealism (René Magritte) as well as the posters of Henri Toulouse-Lautrec *(Tue–Sun 11.30am–5pm | admission 7 euros | rue Jean Van Volsem 71 | www. museedixelles.be)*. Rue du Collège and rue Malibran with shops serving the Portuguese and Moroccan immigrant communities lead to place Flagey. Beneath chestnut trees on the corner of rue des Cygnes, there is a monument to the Portuguese explorer, Fernando Pessoa, while on the other side of the road there is a memorial sculpture dedicated to the heroes of Charles De Coster's Tyll Ulenspiegel .

Like the bow of a luxury liner, the yellow Art Deco building of the old INR broadcasting studios, complete with telecoms tower, overlooks the city. Different types of concerts, sometimes in the afternoon, are staged in the grand rooms of what is now the Flagey → p. 80 Sound and Vision Factory. Café Belga → p. 76 stocks a wide range of international newspapers on the ground floor, and is a popular meeting place. To the left, on the sunnier side, beside rue des Éperons d'Or, are the delightful lakes, known as the Étangs d'Ixelles → p. 46, where joggers, strollers and even anglers create a lively atmosphere. Running down the right bank is avenue du Général de Gaulle, lined by some fine Art Nouveau houses (no. 38 and no. 40). At this point Art Nouveau fans might like to take another slight detour, this time into rue de la Vallée (nos. 18–22 and 29–31) and to rue Vilain XIIII (nos. 9–11), where there are more houses designed by pupils of

Brussels, and then lead to the start of avenue Roosevelt. Striking monuments to Belgian airmen and the industrialist, Ernest Solvay, look down over the boulevard. The next eye-catching feature between the numerous stately ambassadors' residences and the private clubs for members of Brussels' high society is the Free University of Brussels (Université Libre de Bruxelles | no. 50), founded

The old INR radio station behind the lake in the Parc d'Étangs d'Ixelles

Victor Horta, complete with wrought ironwork and glass windows. It doesn't matter whether you walk along the left bank or right bank of the lakes, at the end you will come to Abbaye de la Cambre. This prestigious convent was founded in 1200, but today in the classical wings of La Cambre École Supérieure des Arts Visuels, the designers and fashion gurus of tomorrow are learning their trade.

Behind the Gothic church is the source of the Maelbeek river, which feeds the lakes. Steps take you through elegant gardens, which date from the early 18th century and are among the oldest in

in 1834 by the freemasons. In front of the old library stands the Brabantine neo-Baroque style statue of its founder, Pierre-Théodore Verhaegen. Opposite is a monument to the Catalan teacher and anarchist Francisco Ferrer. Vast expanses of lawn surround the Maison Delune (no. 86), a stately Art Nouveau villa designed by the Belgian architect Léon Delune.

The extensive Villa Empain → p. 54 (no. 67), built in 1931 by Michel Polak for a leading industrialist, is considered to be one of the finest examples of Art Deco. Baron Empain took advantage of the poor railway infrastructure in

Belgium and his companies later developed several railway lines in France, including the Paris metro. Since 2010, this mansion has been the home of the Boghossian Foundation, whose aim is to foster a rapprochement between western and eastern cultures. Avenue Paul Héger, which cuts right through the lively campus, leads into avenue de l'Université, which ends at the **Cimetière d'Ixelles** (daily 8am–4.45pm). This is the final resting place of local heroes, such as the founder of Art Nouveau Victor Horta, the industrialist Ernest Solvay (in an Art Nouveau tomb designed by Victor Horta), the sculptor Constantin Meunier, the violin virtuoso Eugène Ysaye, the author of Ulenspiegel Charles De Coster as well as many other well-known exiles. Outside the entrance to the cemetery, there are a number of student bars, where you will find a wide range of welcome liquid refreshments.

3 GLASS PALACES AND ART NOUVEAU HOUSES

Glittering glass palaces house the institutions of the EU, putting Brussels' Triumphal Arch and the fine Art Nouveau houses in the shade. Allow yourself two hours for this walk, not including museum visits.

Rue Vautier and its front gardens has a distinctly English feel to it. On a sharp bend are the entrances to the **Musée des Sciences Naturelles → p. 43**, which boasts an impressive collection of dinosaur skeletons, and also the **Musée Antoine Wiertz**, formerly the studio of the eccentric painter. Wiertz never received the full measure of recognition that he felt his genius deserved. His paintings are often huge, matching his ambition and ego (no. 62 | Tue–Fri 10am–noon and 1pm–5pm | admission free). The adjacent street, **rue Wiertz**, is dwarfed by the debating chamber of the **European**

Rue Vautier – the front gardens give the street an almost English feel

Parliament, with its elegant curves. Individual visits with a multi-media guide are free *(Mon–Thu 10am and 3pm, Fri 10am)*; visitors wishing to enter during plenary sessions must be part of a guided tour. They will be asked for identification at the entrance *(tel. 0 22 84 21 11 | www. europarl.europa.eu)*. Opposite, office blocks rise in ever-increasing numbers. Located beneath the arcade *(no. 60 rue Wiertz)* is the InfoPoint for the European Parliament.

It is well worth taking a stroll from rue Belliard through the Parc Léopold. On a sloping ridge there are some fine buildings in neoclassical, Art Nouveau and Art Deco styles. Today the park, landscaped in English style, is an oasis of tranquillity in an otherwise vibrant European Quarter. Below the park, chaussée d'Etterbeek leads to the attractive place Jourdan, where there are a number of friendly bars and also a very popular INSIDER TIP friterie. Continue through rue Froissart. Towering above everything on the left is the pink-hued marble building housing what is known as the Consilium, the EU Council of Ministers. At rond-point Schuman cross rue de la Loi. You will see before you Berlaymont → p. 43, the seat of the EU Commission.

The nearest building below in rue de la Loi is the Charlemagne designed by Helmut Jahn, another fine edifice with elegant contours. A short walk takes you down from rue de la Loi to chaussée d'Etterbeek. The right side ends at square Marie-Louise with a lake, fountain garden and grottoes. Art Nouveau architect Victor Horta designed the house at no. 3 as a private clinic. Opposite *(4 avenue Palmerston)* he built the Hôtel van Eetvelde for Leopold II's Minister of the Colonies, and extended it on the left around the Hôtel Delhaye. A little further on at 11 square Ambiorix

you can see the wrought-iron tendrils of Gustave Strauven's Art Nouveau Maison Saint-Cyr. The walk carries on through neat gardens, open for the enjoyment of both EU staff and visitors, to the busy INSIDER TIP *rue Archimède*, vibrant with restaurants, pubs (the James Joyce is Brussels' oldest Irish pub) and shops serving many different communities. At the opposite end rue de la Loi meets the Schuman roundabout. Against the background of the grand Triumphal Arch and the splendour of the museums, there stands a garlanded bust of the EU's founding father, Robert Schuman.

The shady avenue which branches off to the left of the Parc du Cinquantenaire → p. 44, leads to the Pavillon des Passions Humaines or Temple of Human Passions. This, the first building by the Art Nouveau architect Victor Horta, houses an enormous marble relief. The naked figures depicted on it are the cause of as much controversy today as they were when it was first unveiled. After a long period of reconstruction work carried out at the expense of Saudi Arabia, the Great Mosque, designed by the Tunisian architect Boubaker, was opened in 1978 right next to the pavilion. Out of respect the pavilion was then closed and now the relief can only be viewed by peering through the key-hole. A point on the eastern side of the park diagonally opposite the entrance to the museums marks the start of rue des Francs. Gleaming brightly even from a distance is the partially gilded facade of the Maison Cauchie → p. 43, a rare example of a more angular Art Nouveau style. Opposite the pointed tip with fountain at the end of the Parc du Cinquantenaire are several smart, terraced bars, any of which would be perfect for a refreshing drink after your walk.

TRAVEL WITH KIDS

Brussels is very child friendly. There are a lot of fun things to do, many of them free of charge. The larger museums offer engaging, creative workshops, but usually in French or Dutch. But as is often the case in Brussels, English is spoken widely.

ADVENTURE PLAYGROUND
(129 F2) (*∅ O*)

Children love to let off steam on the wide range of play equipment, which includes slide, propeller aircraft, wood cabins and tree trunks, plus tables and chairs for a picnic. *Forêt de Soignes | tram 94: Boitsfort Gare, then down chemin des Silex and back up avenue des Deux Montagnes (railway underpass)*

BOZARSUNDAYS, GOOD MORNING
(126 A4) (*∅ G–H3*)

The *Palais des Beaux-Arts* welcomes families every Sunday morning for breakfast, followed by a child-appropriate guided tour and a concert for children and parents. *Sun 10am–noon | adults 11 euros, children under 12 years of age 4 euros breakfast included | rue Ravenstein 23 | www.bozar.be | metro 1, 5: Gare Centrale*

BRUSK SKATEPARK (125 E5) (*∅ G4*)

Children from the age of 6 can show off their skills and learn new ones at this skateboarding extravaganza. Courses and loan of boards, helmets and knee protectors free of charge at introductory courses March–June and Sept–Oct Wed from 2.30pm and Sat from 11am. *Open at all times | place des Ursulines (opposite Église de la Chapelle) | www.brusk.be | bus 48: Chapelle*

CHEZ LÉON (125 E3) (*∅ G3*)

At this traditional brasserie specialising in Belgian dishes, in particular moules-frites, but which also serves salads, children under 12 eat free. *Daily 11am–11pm | rue des Bouchers 18 | tel. 0 25 11 14 15 | www.chezleon.be | metro: De Brouckère*

CANAL TOUR (123 E6) (*∅ F1*)

Seeing Brussels from the water is not just fun for children. Circular tours on the canal introduce visitors to a completely different side of the city. *May–June, Sept Tue, Wed, Sun 2pm–4pm, July/Aug Tue–Sun noon–5pm | adults 4 euros, children from 3 years 3 euros | quai Béco, place Sainctelette | www.brusselsbywater.be | metro 2, 6: Yser*

MUSEÉ DU JOUET (126 B2) (*∅ H2*)

With no fewer than 33 rooms in the hands-on Toy Museum, the message is look and play. The Théâtre de marion-

A family breakfast in a museum, plus other attractions, which will appeal (not just) to younger visitors

nettes or puppet theatre programme, which runs during the school holidays, is worth investigating.

Daily 10am–noon and 2pm–6pm | adults 5.50 euros, children from 4 years 4.50 euros | rue de l'Association 24 | www. museedujouet.eu | metro 2, 6: Madou

MUSÉE DES SCIENCES NATURELLES
(126–127 C–D6) (ⓜ J4)

Small cabins, animations, interactive games, dinosaur section are among the attractions on offer in the children's rooms at the Natural Sciences Institute. The exhibitions are also tailor-made for children, with some topics in English. The PaleoLab gives children 45 minutes to explore the lost world as a palaeontologist (next to the dinosaur gallery). Younger children will love to eat in the Dino Café. *Tue–Fri 9.30am–5pm, Sat and Sun 10am–6pm, PaleoLab Wed 2.30pm, Sat and Sun 1.30pm, 2.30pm and 3.30pm | adults 7 euros, children under 6 years free of charge, 6 to 8 years 4.50 euros, PaleoLab an additional 2 euros | rue Vautier 29 | www. sciencesnaturelles.be | bus 80: Idalie*

OCÉADE ● (120 C3) (ⓜ O)

Rides at this sub-tropical amusement park near the Atomium include pools, eleven slides, a climbing wall in a waterfall, wave machine, sauna and there's also the Aqua Fun House for younger children. *April–Jun Tue–Fri 10am–6pm, Sat and Sun 10am–9pm, July–Aug daily 10am–9pm, Sept–March Wed–Fri 10am–6pm, Sat and Sun 10am–9pm | admission 16.50 euros, children under 1.30 m 13.50 euros, under 1.15 m free of charge | av. du Football et du Championnat 3 | www. oceade.be | metro 6: Heysel*

ZAABÄR (127 E3) (ⓜ G6)

A chocolate factory where visitors can see how the delicious brown stuff is produced with added flavourings – from behind a glass wall. *Chaussée de Charleroi 125 | tel. 025 33 95 80 | www.zaabar.be | tram 92: Faider*

FESTIVALS & EVENTS

As you would expect in a city renowned for its liberal attitudes, religious celebrations usually stay within the church. It's a cosmopolitan place dedicated to the here and now, sometimes down-to-earth, sometimes the height of elegance.

PUBLIC HOLIDAYS

1 Jan *(New Year's Day);* **Easter Monday; 1 May** *(May Day);* **Ascension Day; Whit Monday; 21 July** *(Belgian national holiday);* **15 Aug** *(Feast of the Assumption);* **1 Nov** *(All Saints Day);* **11 Nov** *(Armistice Day 1918);* **Christmas Day**

EVENTS

JANUARY
▶ *Antiques fair.* Tour et Taxis Exhibition Centre, near place Rogier – top-quality goods

FEBRUARY
▶ *Foire Internationale du Livre.* Book fair with many readings, Tour et Taxis

MARCH
▶ *Eurantica.* Popular antiques fair, Heysel
▶ *Pistes de lancement.* Large circus festival for new groups (even years only)

APRIL
▶ *Art Brussels.* Trade fair for contemporary art, Heysel

MAY
▶ *Kunsten FESTIVAL des Arts.* International avant-garde theatre and dance, Beursschouwburg
▶ *Les Nuits Botanique.* International chanson and pop festival. Le Botanique cultural centre
▶ *Queen Elisabeth International Music Competition of Belgium.* Traditional competition for top musicians. Royal Conservatory of Brussels/Palais des Beaux-Arts
▶ *Jazz-Marathon.* Three days and three nights of jazz on the city's squares and in late-night cafés. Low-cost pass for all venues
▶ ★ *Zinneke Parade.* A colourful, multicultural parade in the city centre; even years only

JUNE
▶ ★ *Bruneaf.* Open days at 70 galleries specialising in non-European art, with respected, foreign dealers invited. Place du Grand Sablon
▶ *Couleur-Café.* Festival of world music. Last weekend of the month, Tour et Taxis

Brussels is a city that loves to party – celebrations usually take the form of festivals and parades, often with dance, drama and music

JULY

▶ ⭐ *Ommegang.* Colourful procession and tournaments on the Grand' Place. Start of the month

▶ *Cinédécouvertes.* Film classics, old and new, cinemathèque

▶ *Conservatoire Royal de Musique.* Every lunch-time until the end of August concerts held in the Baroque Église des Minimes

▶ ● *Bruxelles les Bains.* A large sandy beach is created on place Sainctelette by the canal, with sport, music and miscellany (until the second half of the month)

▶ *21 July (National holiday).* Grand festival and fireworks by the Palais du Roi

AUGUST

▶ *Flower carpet* (even years only). Grand' Place

▶ *Festival Bellone-Brigittines.* Avant-garde dance and music in the Chapelle des Brigittines

▶ *Fiesta latina.* Latin American party with hot rhythms on place du Châtelain

▶ *Memorial Ivo van Damme.* Athletics meeting in the Stade Roi Baudouin

SEPTEMBER

▶ *Europalia.* European arts festival to celebrate one invited country's cultural heritage (2013 India), Palais des Beaux-Arts

▶ INSIDERTIP *Journées du Patrimoine.* 100 historic monuments opened up to the public (some for the only time in the year); on the third weekend

OCTOBER

▶ *Modo brussels.* Creations by young fashion designers from Brussels at various locations

NOVEMBER

▶ *Les Nocturnes du Sablon.* Open days for antiques dealers on place du Grand Sablon

DECEMBER

▶ *Plaisirs d'hiver.* Winter market with specialist stalls and ice-skating rink, between the Grand' Place and Marché aux Poissons

LINKS, BLOGS, APPS & MORE

LINKS

▶ www.cityplug.be An almost complete listing of anything a short- or long-term visitor could need, with reviews in English

▶ www.monarchie.be/en The Belgian monarchy is very much alive – the background story to the entire royal family from King Albert II to Princess Claire

▶ www.beercapital.be Everything about Belgian and Brussels beers and their production methods

▶ www.modobrussels.be What's going on in the Brussels fashion world

▶ www.brusselsartnouveau.be Lots of background information on the Art Nouveau movement, including walking map for visiting the various sights

▶ www.latribunedebruxelles.be Only in French, but with the latest news about Brussels – with blog

▶ www.ebrusselshotels.com A good website for checking out hotels and restaurants in Brussels – with online booking option

FOTOS & VIDEOS

▶ www.bruxelles.be/artdet.cfm?id=4959 Photos of current events, lots of postings from site visitors

▶ www.reflexcity.net Great photos from all quarters of Brussels, plus computer-generated pictures of a better future

▶ www.abconcerts.be/en/abtv Live performances by the best (Belgian) chansonniers, pop and rock groups.

▶ www.youtube.com/watch?v=SM1nN8syhjQ Video about the main places of interest and about shopping in Brussels

▶ www.cityzeum.com/top-videos/bruxelles/1 Evocative videos about the city and its people

▶ www.moodio.tv Web TV with music videos of chansons, pop and rock

Regardless of whether you are still preparing your trip or already in Brussels: these addresses will provide you with more information, videos and networks to make your holiday even more enjoyable

▶ www.expat-blog.com/forum/viewforum.php?id=256 Forum for English-speakers who have made Brussels their second home

▶ blog.lesoir.be In French but with many links to the best bloggers in Belgium

▶ www.bxlblog.be The most detailed blog about everyday life in Brussels, from thoughts about the metro to new cafés – only in French

▶ Le Soir App for Brussels' daily newspaper Le Soir, several updates throughout the day

▶ Localiser ma voiture A simple application that uses GPS location services to help you find your car. You will never forget where you parked

▶ Comic Strips in Brussels PRO Use this app to explore Brussels through the eyes of your favourite comic character

▶ City of Brussels This app is designed for people new to the city and can be downloaded free of charge – lots of maps, information about current events and access to three webcams

▶ www.internations.org/brussels-expats New arrivals in Brussels from all over the world share their experiences and use the site to arrange weekend activities or meet up at events

▶ www.spottedbylocals.com/brussels All the latest information, photos and blogs supplied by the 'natives'

▶ fr-fr.facebook.com/visitbrussels.be Partly in French, partly in English, a site for exchanging news and information

ARRIVAL

If arriving on the E 40 (Bruges), E 34 (Eindhoven–Antwerp) or E 411 (Luxembourg–Namur) motorways, follow signs to Bruxelles Centre. There are plenty of multi-storey and underground carparks in the Lower Town and Upper Town.

The Eurostar to Brussels leaves from London St Pancras International. Trains stop only at Bruxelles-Midi. Pick up metro and tram connections from here. If you wish to purchase rail tickets, visit *www.b-rail.be*

Scheduled flights arrive and depart from Bruxelles-National Aéroport, 15km (9 miles) north-east of the city. Connections to the city: The Brussels Airport Express train service runs to the city centre every 20 minutes between 5.30am and 0.20am. Stops: Bruxelles-Nord, Bruxelles-Central, Bruxelles-Midi. Journey time: 20–30 minutes. Fare: single 2nd class 5.10 euros, 1st class 6.50 euros. If you purchase your ticket on the train, then a surcharge of 3 euros is payable. When returning home, aim to arrive at the airport at least 2 hours before departure time, as baggage and security checks can take some time. For information on delays and cancellations, check with your airline at *www.brusselsairport.be.*

Express buses (no. 12), run by the city's public transport company (STIB), operate every 20 to 30 minutes between 5.30am and 8pm Mon–Fri. Journey time approx. 45 minutes. Stops: Nato, Germinal, Genève, Diamant (change to trams 23 or 24), Schuman (change to metro 1, 5), Luxembourg, Trône (change to metro 2). A single ticket costs 3 euros if obtained from a ticket machine, 5 euros from the driver. A new ticket must be purchased if changing to a different bus/tram/metro line. Single journey 1.80 euros at a machine, 2 euros from the bus/tram driver. From 8pm–midnight and on Saturday, Sunday and public holidays, the airport buses show no. 21.

BANKS & MONEY

Opening times 9am–4pm. Banks in suburban districts often close at lunch-time. There are ATM machines throughout the city. Credit cards are accepted almost everywhere.

BRUSSELS CARD

This card grants free admission to 30 museums and free use of the public transport network. It is available from tourist offices, museums and metro sta-

RESPONSIBLE TRAVEL

It doesn't take a lot to be environmentally friendly whilst travelling. Don't just think about your carbon footprint whilst flying to and from your holiday destination but also about how you can protect nature and culture abroad. As a tourist it is especially important to respect nature, look out for local products, cycle instead of driving, save water and much more. If you would like to find out more about eco-tourism please visit: *www.ecotourism.org*

From arrival to weather

Holiday from start to finish: the most important addresses and information for your trip to Brussels

tions. 24 hours cost 24 euros, 48 hours 34 euros and 72 hours 40 euros. *www. brusselsmuseums.be*

CITY TOURS

ALTERNATIVE CITY TOURS
The Atelier de Recherche et d'Action Urbaines (ARAU), an organisation of alternative architects and urban planners, runs walking tours, which cast a critical eye over various quarters *(bd. Adolphe Max 55 | tel. 0 22 19 33 45 | www.arau.org)*. Itinéraires follows in the footsteps of famous composers, painters and writers, who spent some of their time in Brussels *(rue Hôtel des Monnaies 157 | tel. 0 25 34 30 00 | www. itineraires.be)*. Pro Vélo organises cycle tours through Brussels *(rue de Londres 15 | tel. 0 25 02 73 55 | www.provelo.org)*.

CITY TOURS
Blue buses with a yellow eye cover the main sights. With guide: *Departs daily 10am and 2pm | rue de la Colline 8 (off the Grand' Place) | 27 euros.* No guide but with an option to interrupt or rejoin tour at the designated stops. *Departure every half hour 10am–4pm at the main entrance to the Gare Centrale | 18 euros. Information: Deboeck | tel. 0 25 13 77 44 | www.brussels-city-tours.com*

CLIMATE, WHEN TO GO
Brussels is only approx. 100km (70 miles) from the English Channel. Warm air from Gulf Stream generally ensures a maritime, i.e. mild, but wet climate. Snow doesn't usually last long and in the summer temperatures rarely stay high for extended periods.

tel. weather forecast: Info-Meteo | tel. (*) 0900 2 70 03 | www.meteo.be

CONSULATES & EMBASSIES

UK EMBASSY
Avenue d'Auderghem 10 | Oudergemlaan 10 | tel. 3 22 287 6244 | Mon–Fri 9am–5.30pm | www.ukinbelgium.fco.gov.uk

US EMBASSY
Regentlaan 27 Boulevard du Régent | B-1000 Brussels | tel. 3 22 811 4000 | Mon–Fri 9am–6pm | www.belgium. usembassy.gov

BUDGETING

Coffee	3.50 euros for one cup
Opera	10–180 euros for one ticket
Beer	From 3.50 euros for one glass of gueuze
French fries	2.50 euros for a bag of French fries
Cinema	12 euros for one ticket
Taxi	9 euros Gare du Midi – Grand' Place

CUSTOMS
If travelling within the EU, you may import and export goods intended for personal use free of charge. Upper limits only apply to tobacco (800 cigarettes per adult), wine (90 litres) and spirits (10 l). US citizens are subject to much stricter

regulations. They may only carry a maximum of 200 cigarettes, 2 litres of alcoholic drinks below 15 percent and 1 litre of alcohol drinks over 15 percent.

CYCLE HIRE

Some 2,500 cycles are available for hire at 180 strategic spots throughout the city, e.g. Gare Centrale, place de Brouckère. The basic charge is 1.50 euros; the first half hour costs 0.50 euros, every subsequent hour 2 euros. Users pay by credit card. Information: *www.villo.be*

EMERGENCIES

Ambulance, fire brigade: tel. *100*
Police: tel. *101*

EVENTS CALENDAR

The Wednesday edition of the largest-circulation Brussels daily newspaper Le Soir provides the most detailed listing service (1 euro). The weekly English-language magazine *The Bulletin (What's On)* is published every Thursday (3 euros) and is another useful source of information. Try *www.agenda.be* for online information.

HEALTH

The European Health Insurance Card (EHIC) is accepted in Belgium. In urgent cases the *Hôpital Saint-Pierre (urgences), rue Haute*, will provide treatment free of charge. If you need a chemist *(pharmacie)*, look out for the green neon cross. They are usually open from 9am to 6pm. A box at the entrance to the chemist contains information about night-time and weekend opening hours *(service de garde)*. Emergency doctors: tel. *0 24 79 18 18* | Emergency dentists: tel. *0 24 26 10 26*

INFORMATION BEFORE YOUR JOURNEY

BELGIAN TOURIST OFFICE
217 Marsh Wall, London E14 9FJ | tel. 0207 537 1132 (live operator), 0800 9545 245 (for brochures) | www.belgiumtheplaceto. be
220 East 42nd Street, Suite 3402 | 34th Floor, between 2nd and 3rd Avenue | New York, NY 10017 | tel. 212 75 88 130 | www. visitbelgium.com

INFORMATION IN BRUSSELS

TOURISME INFORMATION BRUXELLES (TIB)
If you wish to book a guided tour, a hotel room, purchase concert and theatre tickets in advance, etc. or day tickets for the metro/trams, there are three tourist information offices:
Town Hall | Grand' Place | Mon–Sat 9am–6pm, Sun 9am–6pm (summer), 10am–2pm (winter) | tel. +32 2 5 13 89 40 | www. visitbrussels.be
Gare du Midi (on the concourse opposite platform 8) | daily 8am–8pm (summer), Mon–Thu 8am–5pm, Fri 8am–8pm, Sat 9am–6pm, Sun 9am–2pm (winter). For information and hotel rooms
Aéroport National (arrivals) | daily 8am–9pm. For information and hotel rooms

BIP (BRUSSELS INFO PLACE)
As well as providing masses of information on guided tours, pre-booking of concert and theatre tickets, the BIP also stages changing photo exhibitions and has a well-stocked bookshop with many books about Brussels. *Rue Royale 2–4 | daily 10am–6pm | tel. 0 25 63 63 99 | www.biponline.be*

ROOMS
Belgian Tourist Reservations | tel. +32 2 5 13 74 84 | www.bruxelles-tourisme.be
To book rooms online visit *www.brussels*

hotels.com or www.hotels-direct-brussels.com (hotel reservations with discounts).

PARKING & SPEED RESTRICTIONS

There are numerous, well-signposted car-parks in Brussels. Charges here are calculated at 2.30 euros per hour, per day (24 hours) 18 euros. At other places where a fee is payable, the charge is based on 0.15 euros for 6 minutes. Often the maximum parking period is restricted to 2 hours. In many urban areas between 6pm and 8am only residents with official permits are allowed to park on the road. Throughout the inner city area of Brussels, there is a speed limit of 30kmph. Elsewhere in the greater Brussels area, this limit may also apply to certain areas, such as near schools, retirement homes or hospitals. Radar cameras enforce compliance. Appeals and fines are handled by the Service Public Fêdéral Justice. Do not in any circumstances leave valuables or items of clothing visible in your car.

PHONE & MOBILE PHONE

The prefix for calls to the UK is 0044, to the USA 001. The code for calling Belgium from abroad is 0032. The local area code for Brussels (02) is part of the number you are dialling, but when calling from abroad, omit the first zero. If you have a pre-paid SIM card for Belgium, then there are no charges for incoming calls. Cheap pre-paid cards are available before you travel at www.travelsimshop.com. Depending on the number of calls you are likely to make, a Pay & Go International package from Proximus (www.proximus.be) may prove to be a cheaper option. If you are planning to stay for a longer period, it is well worth doing some research, perhaps by visit-

Brussels lace – an intricate craft with a long tradition

ing a consumer website, such as www.test-achats.be. Take care with numbers which start with 070, 071 and 090, 091 or 0900. These are not 'toll-free', in fact sometimes they are very expensive.

POST

Post offices are open Mon–Fri 9am–5pm. The central post office (bd. Anspach 1) is also open Sat 10.30am–4.30pm. The post office at Gare du Midi opens for longer: Mon–Fri 7am–7pm and Sat 10.30am–4.30pm (av. Fonsny 32). Inland letters and post-cards cost 0.61 euros, letters and post-cards within the EU 0.93 euros, letters and post-cards outside the EU 1.10. www.bpost.be

PUBLIC TRANSPORT

The metro and the tram are the fastest and most convenient forms of transport. Metro stations are clearly marked by a large, white M on a blue background. Tram and bus-stops have red and white signs. Tickets for the metro are available at station entrances from what are known as GO machines (pay with cash or by credit card). Before boarding you must validate your ticket in one of the orange-coloured machines. Single tickets for the tram and bus may also be purchased from the driver. They will then cost 2 euros, as opposed to 1.80 euros from a machine. Please keep small change to hand and avoid paying with high-denomination notes. Tickets must be validated in one of the orange-coloured machines in the tram or bus and are valid for one hour. Please note: If you change lines, your ticket must once again be inserted into the orange machine. You will then see the remark 'Transit'. If you fail to do this, you risk having to pay a fine of between 8 and 86 euros.

Metro and tram services run between 5.30am and midnight, buses between 5.30am and 1am. Noctis night bus service 0.30am–3pm Fri and Sat, single ticket 3 euros. Some routes and numbers change in the evening.

A single ticket, which entitles the holder to change lines, costs 1.80 euros. A 10-ticket carnet (12.50 euros) is a much cheaper option. Alternatively you could buy a day ticket *(carte jump 1 jour)* for 4.50 euros or a three-day ticket for 9.50 euros. If you are staying in the city for a longer period, a MOBIB ticket works out as a much cheaper alternative. They can be obtained at a one of the public transport network's sales points (there's one at every larger metro station) and a passport-type photo is required. There is a registration fee of 5 euros for a MOBIB ticket, but it is valid for five years. The chip on the ticket can be topped up at the GO machines. MOBIB tickets are validated at metro station barriers or on the white circle in the red boxes on trams and buses. More information and free network maps are available at the Gare du Midi, Gare du Nord, Rogier and Porte de Namur. *Information: www.stib.be*

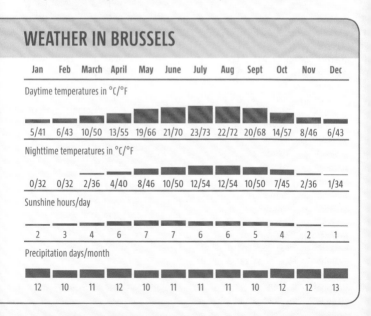

WEATHER IN BRUSSELS

	Jan	Feb	March	April	May	June	July	Aug	Sept	Oct	Nov	Dec
Daytime temperatures in °C/°F	5/41	6/43	10/50	13/55	19/66	21/70	23/73	22/72	20/68	14/57	8/46	6/43
Nighttime temperatures in °C/°F	0/32	0/32	2/36	4/40	8/46	10/50	12/54	12/54	10/50	7/45	2/36	1/34
Sunshine hours/day	2	3	4	6	7	7	6	6	5	4	2	1
Precipitation days/month	12	10	11	12	10	11	11	11	10	12	12	13

TAXIS

Taxis stop when hailed, as long as the Roman numeral I on the roof sign is illuminated. A no. II indicates that it is occupied. Taxis come in all shapes and sizes without any markings on the car doors so look out for the white, yellow and blue triangular stand at the top to spot one on the street. The basic price is 2.40 euros (night supplement 2 euros), every kilometre 1.50 euros within the city limits (2.70 euros for journeys to suburbs outside the 19 districts of Brussels).

Waiting time is included in the price. As soon as the taxi is travelling at less than 20kmph or stops altogether, the meter automatically switches to the waiting tariff of 30 euros per hour. *Taxis bleus | tel. 0 22 68 00 00 | Taxis Verts | tel. 0 23 49 49 49*

THEATRE AND CONCERT TICKETS

Concert, theatre and opera tickets are available from the tourist information office and also at the box offices for the large theatres and concert halls. Tickets for the opera should be booked in advance *(www. lamonnaie.be)*, likewise for concerts in the Palais des Beaux-Arts *(www.bozar.be)*. For young people: Flyers with information on the hottest events are to be found in the foyer of the *Ancienne Belgique (boulevard Anspach 110)*. FNAC *(City 2 | rue Neuve | 2nd floor | Mon–Sat 10am–7pm | tel. (*) 0 90 00 06 00 | www.fnac.be)* always provides a reliable service. Advance purchase online: *www.ticketnet.be.*

TIPPING

Restaurants and cafés apply inclusive prices, i.e. a 17 percent service charge is part of the bill. Small tips are usual only when paying cash. Ushers at the opera, concert halls and theatres never expect tips, in the cinema perhaps 0.50 euros.

WIFI & INTERNET CAFÉS

All Brussels train stations have hotspots for wireless internet access. One hour of surfing costs 7.50 euros (payable by credit card). For totally free WiFi access go to the *Campus Plaine* at the Université Libre de Bruxelles (ULB and VUB) *(boulevard du Triomphe/ boulevard de la Plaine | metro 5: Delta, tram 23, 24: Deuxième Lanciers)*. Hotels without a WiFi system are now the exception.

All the main metro stations have internet cafés, e.g. De Brouckère, Rogier and Porte de Namur.

CURRENCY CONVERTER

£	€	€	£
1	1.10	1	0.90
3	3.30	3	2.70
5	5.50	5	4.50
13	14.30	13	11.70
40	44	40	36
75	82.50	75	67.50
120	132	120	108
250	275	250	225
500	550	500	450

$	€	€	$
1	0.70	1	1.40
3	2.10	3	4.20
5	3.50	5	7
13	9.10	13	18.20
40	28	40	56
75	52.50	75	105
120	84	120	168
250	175	250	350
500	350	500	700

For current exchange rates see www.xe.com

USEFUL PHRASES FRENCH

IN BRIEF

Yes/No/Maybe	oui/non/peut-être
Please/Thank you	s'il vous plaît/merci
Good morning!/afternoon!/ evening!/night!	Bonjour!/Bonjour!/ Bonsoir!/Bonne nuit!
Hello!/goodbye!/See you!	Salut!/Au revoir!/Salut!
Excuse me, please	Pardon!
My name is ...	Je m'appelle ...
I'm from ...	Je suis de ...
May I ...?/ Pardon?	Puis-je ...?/Comment?
I would like to .../ have you got ...?	Je voudrais .../ Avez-vous?
How much is ...?	Combien coûte ...?
I (don't) like this	Ça (ne) me plaît (pas).
good/bad/broken	bon/mauvais/cassé
too much/much/little	trop/beaucoup/peu
all/nothing	tout/rien
Help!/Attention!	Au secours/attention
police/fire brigade/ ambulance	police/pompiers/ ambulance
Could you please help me?	Est-ce que vous pourriez m'aider?
Do you speak English?	Parlez-vous anglais?
Do you understand?	Est-ce que vous comprenez?
Could you please ...?	Pourriez vous ... s'il vous plait?
... repeat that	répéter
... speak more slowly	parler plus lentement
... write that down	l'écrire

DATE & TIME

Monday/Tuesday	lundi/mardi
Wednesday/Thursday	mercredi/jeudi
Friday/Saturday/ Sunday	vendredi/samedi/ dimanche
working day/holiday	jour ouvrable/jour férié
today/tomorrow/ yesterday	aujourd'hui /demain/ hier
hour/minute	heure/minute
day/night/week	jour/nuit/semaine
month/year	mois/année
What time is it?	Quelle heure est-t-il?

Tu parles français?

'Do you speak French?' This guide will help you to say the basic words and phrases in French.

It's three o'clock	Il est trois heures
It's half past three.	Il est trois heures et demi
a quarter to four	quatre heures moins le quart

TRAVEL

open/closed	ouvert/fermé
entrance/exit	entrée/sortie
departure/arrival	départ/arrivée
toilets/restrooms /	toilettes/
ladies/gentlemen	femmes/hommes
(no) drinking water	eau (non) potable
Where is ...?/Where are ...?	Où est ...?/Où sont ...?
left/right	à gauche/à droite
straight ahead/back	tout droit/en arrière
close/far	près/loin
bus/tram/underground / taxi/cab	bus/tramway/métro/taxi
stop/cab stand	arrêt/station de taxi
parking lot/parking garage	parking
street map/map	plan de ville/carte routière
train station/harbour/	gare/port/
airport	aéroport
schedule/ticket	horaire/billet
single/return	aller simple/aller-retour
train/track/platform	train/voie/quai
I would like to rent ...	Je voudrais ... louer.
a car/a bicycle/	une voiture/un vélo/
a boat	un bateau
petrol/gas station	station d'essence
petrol/gas / diesel	essence/diesel
breakdown/repair shop	panne/garage

FOOD & DRINK

The menu, please	La carte, s'il vous plaît.
Could I please have ...?	Puis-je avoir ... s'il vous plaît
bottle/carafe/glass	bouteille/carafe/verre
knife/fork/spoon	couteau/fourchette/cuillère
salt/pepper/sugar	sel/poivre/sucre
vinegar/oil	vinaigre/huile
milk/cream/lemon	lait/crême/citron
cold/too salty/not cooked	froid/trop salé/pas cuit

with/without ice/sparkling	avec/sans glaçons/gaz
vegetarian	végétarien(ne)
May I have the bill, please	Je voudrais payer, s'il vous plaît
bill	addition

SHOPPING

pharmacy/chemist	pharmacie/droguerie
baker/market	boulangerie/marché
shopping centre	centre commercial
department store	grand magasin
100 grammes/1 kilo	cent grammes/un kilo
expensive/cheap/price	cher/bon marché/prix
more/less	plus/moins
organically grown	de l'agriculture biologique

ACCOMMODATION

I have booked a room	J'ai réservé une chambre
Do you have any ... left?	Avez-vous encore ...?
single room/double room	chambre simple/double
breakfast	petit déjeuner
half board/	demi-pension/
full board (American plan)	pension complète
shower/sit-down bath	douche/bain
balcony/terrace	balcon /terrasse
key/room card	clé/carte magnétique
luggage/suitcase/bag	bagages/valise/sac

BANKS, MONEY & CREDIT CARDS

bank/ATM/pin code	banque/guichet automatique/code
cash/credit card	comptant/carte de crédit
bill/coin	billet/monnaie

HEALTH

doctor/dentist/	médecin/dentiste/
paediatrician	pédiatre
hospital/emergency clinic	hôpital/urgences
fever/pain	fièvre/douleurs
diarrhoea/nausea	diarrhée/nausée
sunburn	coup de soleil
inflamed/injured	enflammé/blessé
plaster/bandage	pansement/bandage
ointment/pain reliever	pommade/analgésique

POST, TELECOMMUNICATIONS & MEDIA

stamp	timbre
lettre/postcard	lettre/carte postale
I need a landline phone card	J'ai besoin d'une carte téléphonique pour fixe.
I'm looking for a prepaid card for my mobile	Je cherche une recharge pour mon portable.
Where can I find internet access?	Où puis-je trouver un accès à internet?
dial/connection/engaged	composer/connection/occupé
socket/charger	prise électrique/chargeur
computer/battery/rechargeable battery	ordinateur/batterie/accumulateur
at sign (@)	arobase
internet address (URL)/e-mail address	adresse internet/mail
internet connection/wifi	accès internet/wi-fi
e-mail/file/print	mail/fichier/imprimer

LEISURE, SPORTS & BEACH

beach	plage
sunshade/lounger	parasol/transat
low tide/high tide/current	marée basse/marée haute/courant
cable car/chair lift	téléphérique/télésiège
(rescue) hut	refuge

NUMBERS

0	zéro	17	dix-sept
1	un, une	18	dix-huite
2	deux	19	dix-neuf
3	trois	20	vingt
4	quatre	30	trente
5	cinq	40	quarante
6	six	50	cinquante
7	sept	60	soixante
8	huit	70	soixante-dix
9	neuf	80	quatre-vingt
10	dix	90	quatre-vingt-dix
11	onze	100	cent
12	douze	200	deux cents
13	treize	1000	mille
14	quatorze		
15	quinze	½	un[e] demi[e]
16	seize	¼	un quart

USEFUL PHRASES DUTCH

PRONUNCIATION

To help you with the pronunciation we have added to each word or phrase a simplified guide on how to say it [in square brackets]. Here kh denotes a guttural sound similar to 'ch' in Scottish 'loch', and ü is spoken like 'u' in French 'tu'.

IN BRIEF

Yes/No/Maybe	ja [ya]/nee [nay]/misschien [miss-kheen]
Please/	alstublieft [ashtübleeft]/alsjeblieft
Thank you	[ash-yer-bleeft]/bedankt [bedankt]
Excuse me	Sorry [sorry]
May I ...?/ Pardon?	Mag ik ...? [makh ick]/ Pardon? [spoken as in French]
I would like to .../	Ik wil graag ... [ick vill khraakh]/
Have you got ...?	Heeft u ...? [hayft ü]
How much is ...	Hoeveel kost ...? [hoofayl kost]
I (don't) like that	Dat vind ik (niet) leuk. [dat find ick (niet) lurk]
broken/doesn't work	kapot [kapott]/werkt niet [vairkt neet]
Help!/Attention!/	Hulp! [hülp]/Let op! [lett opp]/
Caution!	Voorzichtig!/[forzikhtikh]
Ambulance	ambulance [ambülantser]
Police/Fire brigade	politie [politsee]/brandweer [brandvayr]

GREETINGS, FAREWELL

Good morning!/afternoon!/	Goeden morgen/dag! [khooyer morkhe/dakh]/
evening!/night!	avond!/nacht! [afond/nakht]
Hello!/goodbye!	Hallo! [hallo]/Dag! [daakh]
See you	Doei! [dooee]
My name is ...	Ik heet ... [ick hayt]
What's your name?	Hoe heet u? [hoo hayt ü]/Hoe heet je? [hoo hayt yer]
I'm from ...	Ik kom uit ... [ick komm owt]

DATE AND TIME

Monday/Tuesday	maandag [maandakh]/dinsdag [dinnsdakh]
Wednesday/Thursday	woensdag [voonsdakh]/donderdag [donderdakh]
Friday/Saturday	vrijdach [fraydakh]/zaterdag [zatterdakh]
Sunday/holiday	zondag [zonndakh]/feestdag [faystdakh]

Spreek jij nederlands?

'Do you speak Dutch?' This guide will help you to say the basic words and phrases in Dutch.

today/tomorrow/ yesterday	vandaag [fanndaakh]/morgen (morkher)/ gisteren (khisteren)
What time is it?	Hoe laat is het? (hoo laat iss hett)
It's three o'clock	Het is drie uur [hett iss dree üür]

TRAVEL

open/closed	open [open]/gesloten [khesloten]
entrance	ingang [innkhang]/inrit [inritt]
exit	uitgang [owtkhang]/*(car park)* uitrit [owtritt], *(motorway)* afslag [affslakh]
departure/ arrival	vertrektijd [fertrekktayt]/vertrek [fertrekk]/ aankomst [aankommst]
toilets women/men	toilet [twalett]/dames [daamers]/heren [hayren]
(not) drinking water	(geen) drinkwater [(kheen) drinkvaater]
Where is ...?/Where are ...?	Waar is ...? [vaar iss]/Waar zijn ...? [vaar zayn]
left/right/ straight ahead/ back/close/far	links [links]/rechts [rekhts]/ rechtdoor [rekhtdor]/ terug [terükh]/dichtbij [dikhtbay]/ver [fair]
bus/tram	bus [büs]/tram [tram]
U-underground / taxi/cab	metro [metro] / taxi [taxi]
bus stop/cab stand	station [stasseeonn]/taxistandplaats [taxistandplaats]
parking lot/ parking garage	parkplaats [parkplaats]/ parkeergarage [parkayrkharager]
train station/harbour	station [stasseeonn]/haven [haafen]
airport	luchthaven [lükhthaafen]
timetable/ticket	dienstregeling [dienstraykheling]/kaartje [kaartyer]
single/return	enkel [enkel]/retour [retour]
train / track/platform	trein [trayn] / spoor [spoor]/perron [peronn]
I would like to rent ...	Ik wil graag ... huren [ick vill khraakh ... hüüren]
a car/a bicycle/a boat	een auto [enn owto]/fiets [feets]/boot [boat]
petrol / gas station	tankstation [tankstasseeonn]
petrol/gas / diesel	benzine [benseen]/diesel [diesel]

FOOD & DRINK

Could you please book a table for tonight for four?	Wilt u alstublieft voor vanavond een tafel voor vier personen voor ons reserveren. [villt ü ashtübleeft for fannaafont en taafel for feer pairzonen for ons reservayren]
on the terrace/ by the window	op het terras [opp het terrass]/ bij het raam [bay het raam]
The menu, please	De kaart, alstublieft. [de kaart ashtübleeft]

Could I please have ...?	Mag ik ...? [makh ick]
bottle/carafe/glass	fles [fless]/karaf [karaff]/glas [khlass]
a knife/a fork/a spoon	mes [mess]/fork [fork]/lepel [laypel]
salt/pepper/sugar	zout [zowt]/peper [payper]/suiker [zowker]
vinegar/oil	azijn [azayn]/olie [olee]
with/without ice/sparkling	met [mett]/zonder ijs [zonder ays]/bubbels [bübbels]
May I have the bill, please?	Mag ik afrekenen [makh ick affraykenen]
bill/receipt	rekening [raykening]/bonnetje [bonnetyer]

SHOPPING

Where can I find...?	Waar vind ik...? [vaar finnt ick]
I'd like .../I'm looking for ...	Ik will ... [ick vill]/Ik zoek ... [ick zook]
pharmacy/chemist	apotheek [apotayk]/drogisterij [drookhisteray]
department store	winkelcentrum [vinkelzentrümm]
supermarket	supermarkt [züpermarkt]
100 grammes/1 kilo	1 ons [onz]/1 kilo [kilo]
expensive/cheap/price	duur [düür]/goedkoop [khootkoap]/prijs [prayss]
more/less	meer [mayr]/minder [minder]

ACCOMMODATION

I have booked a single/ double room	Ik heb een eenpersoonskamer/tweepersoonskamer gereserveerd [ick hepp en aynperzoanskaamer/ tvayperzoanskaamer khereservayrt]
Do you have any ... left?	Heeft u nog ... [hayft ü nokh]
breakfast/half board	ontbijt [ontbayt]/halfpension [hallfpenseeonn]
full board (American plan)	volpension [follpenseeonn]
at the front/seafront	naar de voorkant/zee [naar de forkannt/zay]
shower/sit-down bath	douche [doosh]/badkamer [battkaamer]
balcony/terrace	balkon [balkonn]/terras [terrass]
key/room card	sleutel [slurtel]/sleutelkaart [slurtelkaart]

BANKS, MONEY & CREDIT CARDS

bank/ATM	bank [bank]/pinautomat [pinn-owtomaat]
cash/credit card	kontant [kontant]/pinpas [pinnpass]/ creditcard [kreditkaart]

HEALTH

doctor/dentist/ paediatrician	arts [arts]/tandarts [tandarts]/ kinderarts [kinderarts]
hospital/ emergency clinic	ziekenhuis [zeekenhows]/ spoedeisende hulp[spootayzender hülp]
fever/pain	koorts [koorts]/pijn [payn]

diarrhoea/nausea	diaree [diaray]/misselijkheid [misselick-hayt]
inflamed/injured	ontstoken [ontstoaken]/gewond [khevonnt]
pain reliever/tablet	pijnstiller [paynstiller]/tablet [tablett]

POST, TELECOMMUNICATIONS & MEDIA

stamp/letter/ postcard	zegel [zaykhel]/brief [breef]/ aanzichtkaart [aanzikhtkaart]
I need a landline phone card	Ik wil graag een telefoonkaart voor het vaste net. [ick vill khraakh en telephonekaart for het faster net]
I need a prepaid card for my mobile	Ik zoek een prepaid-kaart voor mijn mobieltje. [ick zook en prepaid-kaart for mayn mobeelt-yer]
Where can I find internet access?	Waar krijg ik toegang tot internet [vaar kraykh ick too-khang tot internet]
socket/adapter/ charger	stopcontact [stoppkontakt]/adapter [adapter]/ oplader [oplaader]
computer/battery/ rechargeable battery	computer [computer]/batterij [batteray]/ accu [akkü]
internet connection/wifi	internetverbinding [internetferbinnding]/WLAN
e-mail/file/ print	mail [mail]/bestand [bestant]/ uitdraaien [owtdraa-yen]

LEISURE, SPORTS & BEACH

beach/bathing beach	strand [strand]/strandbad [strandbart]
sunshade/ lounger	zonnescherm [zonner sherm]/ zonnestoel [zonnerstool]
low tide/high tide	laagwater [laakhvaater]/hoogwater [hoakhvaater]

NUMBERS

0	nul [nüll]	15	vijftien [fayfteen]
1	één [ayn]	16	zestien [zesteen]
2	twee [tvay]	17	zeventien [zerventeen]
3	drie [dree]	18	achtien [akhteen]
4	vier [feer]	19	negentien [naykhenteen]
5	vijf [fayf]	70	zeventig [zerventikh]
6	zes [zess]	80	tachtig [takhtikh]
7	zeven [zerven]	90	negentig [naykhentikh]
8	acht [akht]	100	honderd [hondert]
9	negen [naykhen]	200	tweehonderd [tvayhondert]
10	tien [teen]	1000	duizend [dowzent]
11	elf [elf]	2000	tweeduizend [tvaydowzent]
12	twaalf [tvaalf]	10000	tienduizend [teendowzent]
13	dertien [dairteen]	1/2	half [hallf]
14	viertien [feerteen]	1/4	kwart [kvart]

NOTES

FOR YOUR NEXT HOLIDAY ...

MARCO POLO TRAVEL GUIDES

ALGARVE
AMSTERDAM
BARCELONA
BERLIN
BRUSSELS
BUDAPEST
CALIFORNIA
COLOGNE
CORFU
CRETE
DUBAI
DUBROVNIK &
   DALMATIAN
   COAST
EDINBURGH
EGYPT

FINLAND
FLORENCE
FLORIDA
FRENCH RIVIERA
   NICE, CANNES &
   MONACO
IRELAND
ISTANBUL
KOS
LAKE GARDA
LANZAROTE
LONDON

LOS ANGELES
MADEIRA
   PORTO SANTO
MALLORCA
MALTA
   GOZO
NEW YORK
NORWAY
PARIS
RHODES
ROME

SAN FRANCISCO
SICILY
SOUTH AFRICA
STOCKHOLM
THAILAND
TURKEY
   SOUTH COAST
VENICE

MARCO POLO

With ROAD ATLAS & PULL-OUT MAP

LAKE GARDA

MONTE BALDO WITH MOUNTAIN BIKE
cable car in Malcesine takes bikes too

"KISSES" IN SALO
y chocolate "Baceti"

Travel with
Insider Tips

MARCO POLO

NEW YORK

MEADOWS, WILD FLOWERS AND SKYSCRAPERS
een is chic: the High Line in Chelsea

TAIL ON CLOUD NINE
ooftop bar at 230 Fifth Street

Travel with
Insider Tips

MARCO POLO

With ROAD ATLAS & PULL-OUT MAP

FRENCH RIVIERA
NICE, CANNES & MONACO

SPECTACULAR GRAND CANYON DU VERDON
Breath-taking scenery that takes some beating

SNIFFING THE AIR
The perfume manufacturers of Grasse

Travel with
Insider Tips

www.marco-polo.com

MARCO POLO

With STREET ATLAS & PULL-OUT MAP

BERLIN

A STUNNING ISLAND JUST FOR ART
Showcasing treasures from around the world

STAY COOL AT NIGHT
club scene sets the trend

Travel with
Insider Tips

MARCO POLO

With ROAD ATLAS & PULL-OUT MAP

ALLORCA

AN FLAIR IN THE MEDITERRANEAN
Mallorca's most beautiful beach

"IN" CROWD MEET
onda in Deià

Travel with
Insider Tips

- PACKED WITH INSIDER TIPS
- BEST WALKS AND TOURS
- FULL-COLOUR PULL-OUT MAP
  AND STREET ATLAS

STREET ATLAS

The green line ▬▬▬ indicates the Walking tours (p. 90–95)

All tours are also marked on the pull-out map

Photo: Palais du Roi

Exploring Brussels

The map on the back cover shows how the area has been sub-divided

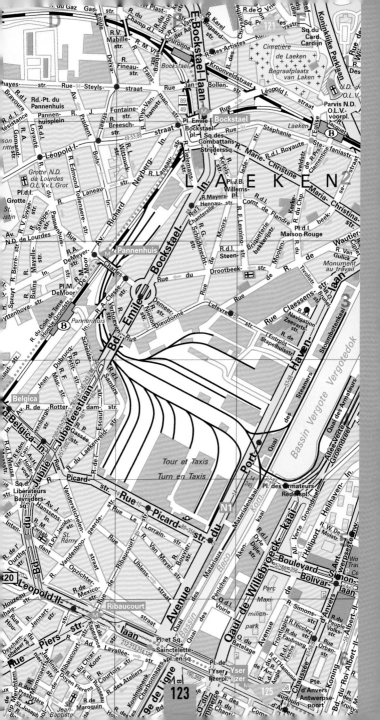

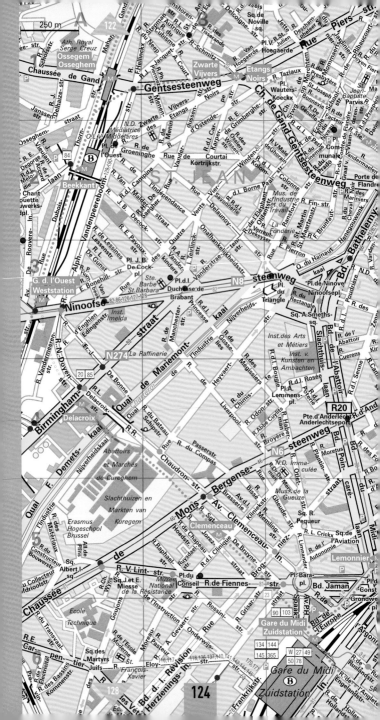

BRUXELLES

127

131

250 m

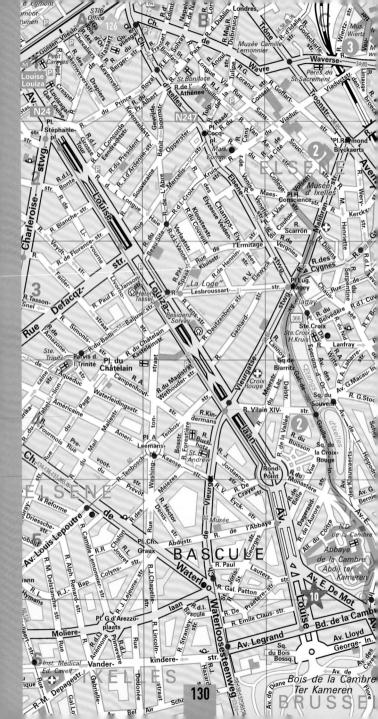

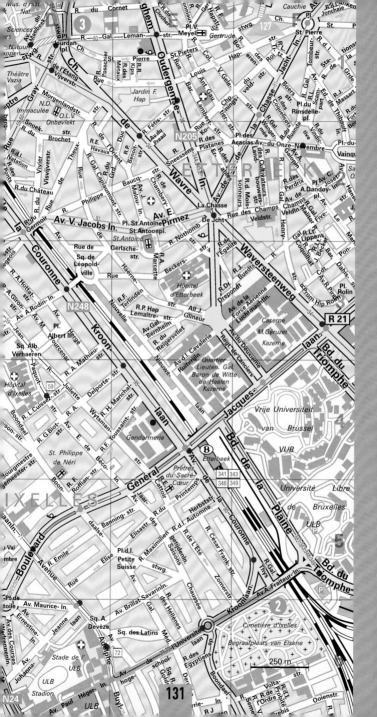

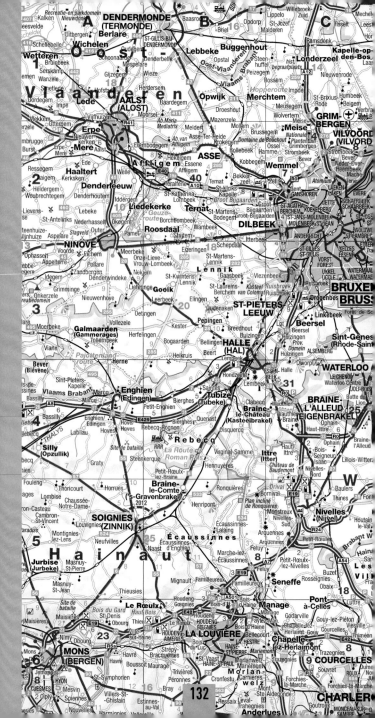

This index lists a selection of the streets and squares shown on the street atlas

KEY TO STREET ATLAS

Autoroute / Autobahn		Autosnelweg / Motorway	
Route à quatre voies / Vierspurige Straße		Weg met vier rijstroken / Road with four lanes	
Route de transit / Durchgangsstraße		Weg voor doorgaand verkeer / Thoroughfare	
Route principale / Hauptstraße		Hoofdweg / Main road	
Autres routes / Sonstige Straßen		Overige wegen / Other roads	
Parking - Information / Parkplatz - Information	P i	Parkeerplaats - Informatie / Parking place - Information	
Rue à sens unique / Einbahnstraße		Straat met eenrichtingsverkeer / One-way street	
Zone piétonne / Fußgängerzone		Voetgangerszone / Pedestrian zone	
Chemin de fer principal avec gare / Hauptbahn mit Bahnhof	B	Belangrijke spoorweg met station / Main railway with station	
Autre ligne / Sonstige Bahn		Overige spoorweg / Other railway	
Métro / U-Bahn	M	Ondergrondse spoorweg / Underground	
Tramway / Straßenbahn		Tram / Tramway	
Ligne d'autobus / Buslinie		Buslijn / Bus-route	
Église remarquable - Autre église / Sehenswerte Kirche - Sonstige Kirche	✚ ✚	Bezienswaardige kerk - Andere kerk / Church of interest - Other church	
Synagogue / Synagoge	✡	Synagoge / Synagogue	
Monument - Auberge de jeunesse / Denkmal - Jugendherberge	Å ▲	Monument - Jeugdherberg / Monument - Youth hostel	
Poste de police - Bureau de poste / Polizeistation - Postamt	● ✆	Politiebureau - Postkantoor / Police station - Post office	
Hôpital / Krankenhaus	✚	Ziekenhuis / Hospital	
Zone bâtie, bâtiment public / Bebaute Fläche, öffentliches Gebäude		Bebouwing, openbaar gebouw / Built-up area, public building	
Zone industrielle / Industriegelände		Industrieterrein / Industrial area	
Parc, bois - Cimetière / Park, Wald - Friedhof	+ + + +	Park, bos - Kerkhof / Park, forest - Cemetery	
Promenades en ville / Stadtspaziergänge		Wandelingen door de stad / Walking tours	
MARCO POLO Highlight	★1	MARCO POLO Highlight	

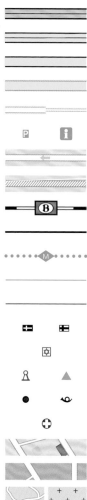

INDEX

This index lists all sights, museums and destinations plus the main squares and streets, the key terms and people featured in this guide. Numbers in bold indicate a main entry.

WRITE TO US

e-mail: info@marcopologuides.co.uk

Did you have a great holiday?
Is there something on your mind?
Whatever it is, let us know!
Whether you want to praise, alert us
to error or give us a personal tip –
MARCO POLO would be pleased to
hear from you.
We do everything we can to provide
the very latest information for your trip.

Nevertheless, despite all of our authors'
thorough research, errors can creep
in. MARCO POLO does not accept any
liability for this. Please contact us by
e-mail or post.

MARCO POLO Travel Publishing Ltd
Pinewood, Chineham Business Park
Crockford Lane, Chineham
Basingstoke, Hampshire RG24 8AL
United Kingdom

PICTURE CREDITS

Cover Photograph: Atomium (Look: age fotostock)
Images: S.-C. Bettinger (1 bottom); DuMont Bildarchiv: Kiedrowski (5, 7, 8), Kluyver (2 centre bottom, 26/27); Eva Luna (16 top); R. Freyer (34, 47, 64 l., 68, 81, 94, 102 top, 118/119); L. Gerbaud (2 top, 4); Getty Images/Stone: Images Etc Ltd (41); Groupe Cible – Solex (16 bottom); © iStockphoto.com: Steven Miric (16 centre), webphotographer (17 bottom); Lacasabxl: Frank Abbeloos (17 top); Laif: Gonzalez (3 bottom, 25, 30, 62, 76, 82/83), Hahn (65, 107), hemis.fr (37, 58, 88), Jung (2 bottom, 56/57), Reporters (61); Laif/hemis.fr: Cintract (2 centre top, 6, 33, 90/91), Degas (78), Maisant (87), Perousse (18/19); Laif/Laif5: Xinhua (98); Laif/Laif23/Photonews: Reynaers (38); Laif/Reporters: Van de Vel (20); Laif/Tripelon: Jarry (71, 84); Look: age fotostock (1 top, 55), Zegers (flap l.); Look/SagaPhoto: Gautier (9); mauritius images: Alamy (24 bottom), FreshFood (64 r.), Mirau (42), Photononstop (23); O.P.T. Office du Tourisme Wallonie: Remy (3 top, 12/13, 15, 32, 49, 66/67, 73, 93, 96, 97, 98/99, 99, 103); picture alliance: R. Kiedrowski (24 top); O. Stadler (flap r., 10/11, 43, 102 bottom); T. Stankiewicz (3 centre, 74/75); Toerisme Vlaanderen (44, 51, 96/97); Toerisme Vlaanderen: A. Kouprianoff (52)

1st Edition 2012

Worldwide Distribution: Marco Polo Travel Publishing Ltd, Pinewood, Chineham Business Park, Crockford Lane, Basingstoke, Hampshire RG24 8AL, United Kingdom. Email: sales@marcopolouk.com
© MAIRDUMONT GmbH & Co. KG, Ostfildern
Chief editors: Michaela Lienemann (concept, managing editor), Marion Zorn (concept, text editor)
Author: Sven-Claude Bettinger; Editor: Karin Liebe
Programme supervision: Ann-Katrin Kutzner, Nikolai Michaelis, Silwen Randebrock
Picture editor: Gabriele Forst, Barbara Schmid
What's hot: wunder media, Munich; Cartography street atlas: © MAIRDUMONT, Ostfildern;
Cartography pull-out map: © MAIRDUMONT, Ostfildern
Design: milchhof : atelier, Berlin; Front cover, pull-out map cover, page 1: factor product munich
Translated from German by Paul Fletcher, Suffolk; editor of the English edition: Tony Halliday, Oxford
Prepress: BW-Medien GmbH, Leonberg
Phrase book in cooperation with Ernst Klett Sprachen GmbH, Stuttgart, Editorial by Pons Wörterbücher

DOS & DON'TS ✍

A few things to bear in mind while in Brussels

DON'T EAT IN THE ILOT SACRÉ QUARTER

Visitors repeatedly fall for the abundant displays of fish and seafood, the inviting interiors, the neat terraces and insistent waiters. The meals are often disappointing and when the bill comes, diners find they are paying highly inflated prices.

DO BOOK A TABLE AT YOUR CHOSEN RESTAURANT

It doesn't matter whether it's a Michelin-starred restaurant or a small brasserie – the Bruxellois like to eat out and do so regularly. So if you know where you want to eat, then it is essential to book your table, and if it's for the weekend, do it a few days in advance. However, it is not normally possible to book a particular table.

DON'T USE YOUR MOBILE PHONE WHILE DRIVING

Unless the car is fitted with a wireless connection, drivers must not use a mobile phone at the wheel. It is a serious offence. If caught, drivers must pay a fine of 100 euros if paid on-the-spot, up to 1,375 euros if the case goes to court.

DON'T PARK ILLEGALLY

Even if the locals park haphazardly on pedestrian crossings and pavements, copying them is not recommended. At weekends, the police will tow away cars without mercy. And that means long waits at the police station, a fine of at least 140 euros, towing costs (from 140 euros) and a taxi ride to the car pound out of town.

DON'T TRUST OTHER DRIVERS

Major roads are clearly marked as priority routes, but Brussels drivers have the rather disagreeable habit of shooting out of side roads, even though they have no right-of-way. An infringement of the give way rule can cost up to 275 euros.

DON'T GET INTO AN UNLICENSED TAXI

Some taxis not licensed by the Brussels regional government will ply for trade, particularly at the airport. So look out for no license plate on the radiator grille, no white, yellow and blue triangular stand on the roof. Otherwise expect extortionate prices.

DON'T TAKE SOFT DRUGS

The Belgian High Court has repealed the country's liberal drug laws. Even if you occasionally pick up the smell of marijuana, smoking and dealing hash is forbidden.

DON'T SMOKE IN A RESTAURANT

Smoking is not allowed in any place where food is served. So many restaurants now have separate smoking rooms. Pubs and bars where only drinks are served must have smoking and non-smoking sections.